Edmund Gosse

Collected Essays

Portraits and Sketches

Edmund Gosse

Collected Essays

Portraits and Sketches

ISBN/EAN: 9783955630676

Auflage: 1

Erscheinungsjahr: 2013

Erscheinungsort: Bremen, Deutschland

@ Leseklassiker in Access Verlag GmbH, Fahrenheitstr. 1, 28359 Bremen. Alle Rechte beim Verlag und bei den jeweiligen Lizenzgebern.

Leseklassiker

PORTRAITS AND SKETCHES

BY

EDMUND GOSSE, C.B.

LONDON
WILLIAM HEINEMANN
1913

TO
H. OF C.
THIS VOLUME IS AFFECTIONATELY
DEDICATED

PREFACE

THESE short studies of authors whom I have known more or less intimately, and have observed with curiosity and admiration, base whatever value they may possess on their independence. They are imperfect, perhaps erroneous, but they are not second-hand. Whether they are the result of a few flashing glimpses, or of the patient scrutiny of many years, in either case they are my own. I hope that some of them, at least, may be found to possess the interest which attaches to even a rude pencil-sketch of a famous person, drawn faithfully from the life.

The persons dealt with are of widely differing importance, and it is probable that posterity will intensify the distinction between them. Some names are here included which history may neglect altogether; here are others which we believe will become more and more luminous with the passage of years. But the men discussed in the following pages had the common characteristic of devotion to literature; all were writers, and each had, in his own time and way, a serious and even a passionate conception of the responsibilities of the art of writing. They were all, in their various capacities, engaged in keeping bright, and in passing on unquenched, the torch of literary tradition.

In the case of such men of letters, there has always seemed to me to be a singular interest in observing how personal character acts upon the work performed. It is less entertaining, for instance, to dwell exclusively on the verses of a poet, or exclusively on the incidents of his life, than to attempt the more complicated study of these elements in inter-relation to one another, as has been done, but only too rarely, in the best critical biographies. M. Paul Desjardins, in an amusing and illuminating phrase, speaks of "la cinématographie d'une abeille dans le mystère de la mellification." This, I confess, is what I like best in a literary biography, and it is what I have attempted to produce. To analyse the honey is one thing, and to dissect the bee another; but I find a special pleasure in watching him, myself unobserved, in the act of building up and filling the cells. In what I have recorded, I have tried to concentrate attention, not on vague anecdotes and empty tricks of conduct, but on such traits of character as throw light on the man's intellect and imagination, and are calculated to help us in the enjoyment of his work. And while I hope I have never courted sensation by recounting anything scandalous, I have not hesitated to tell what I believe to be the truth, nor glossed over peculiarities of temperament when they help us to comprehend the published writings.

Of all the human beings whom I have known,

I think that Algernon Swinburne was the most extraordinary. It is therefore needless to excuse the length of the essay with which this volume opens. Hitherto little that is trustworthy has been published about this amazing man, around whose career a good deal of legend has at one time or another crystallised. He was so much of a hermit of late years that curiosity has been glad to satisfy itself with tales which were picturesque although they were unfounded. I hope to start the work, which others will continue and make perfect, of preserving the true features of Swinburne as a poet and as a person. My recollections of his person and character are limited and imperfect, and no one is more conscious of their imperfection than I am; but so far as I can ensure fidelity to the truth, they are true; and I cannot help hoping that they will be of service to those, perhaps still unborn, who will elaborate the final portrait. Whatever vicissitudes of taste our literature may undergo, one thing appears to me absolutely certain, that Swinburne will end by taking his place as one of the few unchallenged Immortals, about whose personal and intellectual habits no faithful record is unwelcome.

In "Festus" Bailey and "Orion" Horne we have typical products of the transitional period between Shelley and Keats on the one hand and Tennyson and Browning on the other. Those who had an opportunity of conversing with these interesting and pathetic figures in their old age are growing rare, while no life of either of them has appeared.

My recollections of Mandell Creighton were written down before the appearance of the "Life" of him published by his accomplished widow. Mrs. Creighton's view of her husband's character, although so exhaustive and so largely illuminated by documents, was pre-eminently ecclesiastical; I venture to hope that there is therefore still an excuse for preserving the reminiscences of a lay friend, as an appendix to her excellent monument. This is still more the case in respect to Shorthouse, where the official biography, I am bound to confess, seems to me to present not an imperfect so much as a false impression of a very singular person. The great danger of twentieth-century biography is its unwillingness to accept any man's character save at the valuation of his most cautious relatives, and in consequence to reduce all figures to the same smooth forms and the same mediocre proportions.

The last portrait in my little gallery is more obviously unfinished than any of the rest. If the presence of M. André Gide among so many of those who have passed away is objected to, I will say that I like to feel that I take one living friend with me in my round of respectful visits to the dead. His is not a portrait; it is hardly an outline; but I wish to delay no longer in recommending to the study of English readers a fascinating writer, still young, who is destined I believe to take a place in the very first rank of European writers.

September 1912   EDMUND GOSSE

CONTENTS

	PAGE
PREFACE	vii
SWINBURNE	1
PHILIP JAMES BAILEY	59
"ORION" HORNE	95
AUBREY DE VERE	117
A FIRST SIGHT OF TENNYSON	127
A VISIT TO WHITTIER	135
THE AUTHOR OF "JOHN INGLESANT"	149
MANDELL CREIGHTON	163
ANDREW LANG	197
WOLCOTT BALESTIER	213
CARL SNOILSKY	227
EUGÈNE MELCHIOR DE VOGÜÉ	241
ANDRÉ GIDE	267
INDEX	291

SWINBURNE
1837–1909

SWINBURNE

MEN who to-day have not passed middle age can scarcely form an impression of what the name and fame of Algernon Charles Swinburne meant forty years ago to those who were then young and enthusiastic candidates for apprenticeship in the fine arts. Criticism now looks upon his work—and possibly it is right in so looking—rather as closing than as opening a great poetic era. The conception is of a talent which collects all the detonating elements of a previous illumination, and lets them off, once and for all, in a prodigious culminating explosion, after which darkness ensues. But such a conception of Swinburne, as the floriated termination of the romantic edifice, or, once more to change the image, as one who brought up the rear of a long and straggling army, would have seemed to his adorers of 1869 not merely paradoxical but preposterous. It was not doubted by any of his admirers that here they held an incomparable poet of a new order, "the fairest first-born son of fire," who was to inaugurate a new age of lyric gold.

This conception was shared alike by the few who in those days knew him personally, and by the many who did not. While the present writer was still in that outer class, he well remembers being told that an audience of the elect, to whom Swinburne recited the yet unpublished " Dolores," had been moved to such incredible ecstasy by it that several of them had sunk on their knees, then and there, and adored him as a god. Those were blissful times, when poets and painters, if they were attached to Keats' "little clan," might hope for honours which were private indeed, and strictly limited, but almost divine. The extraordinary reputation of Swinburne in the later sixties was constructed of several elements. It was built up on the legend of his mysterious and unprecedented physical appearance, of the astonishing verbal beauty of his writings, but most of all on his defiance of the intellectual and religious prejudices of his age and generation. He was not merely a poet, but a flag; and not merely a flag, but the Red Flag incarnate. There was an idea abroad, and it was not ill-founded, that in matters of taste the age in England had for some time been stationary, if not stagnant. It was necessary to wake people up; as Victor Hugo had said: "Il faut rudoyer le genre humain," and in every gesture it was believed that Swinburne set forth to "rudoyer" the Philistines.

This was welcome to all young persons sitting in bondage, who looked up to Swinburne as to the deliverer. He also enjoyed, in popular belief, the advantage of excessive youth. In point of fact, his immaturity was not so dazzling as was reported by the newspapers, or, alas ! as he then himself reported.

When "Poems and Ballads" appeared he was in his thirtieth year, yet he was generally reported to be only twenty-four. This is interesting merely because there are five or six years of Swinburne's early manhood which seem to be without any visible history. What did he do with himself between 1860, when "The Queen-Mother" was stillborn, and 1865, when he flashed into universal prominence as the author of "Atalanta in Calydon"? On the large scale, nothing; on the small scale, the bibliographer (aided by the indefatigable Mr. Thomas J. Wise) detects the review of Baudelaire's "Fleurs du Mal" in the *Spectator* (1862), and a dim sort of short story in prose called "Dead Love" (1864). No doubt this was a time of tremendous growth in secret; but, visibly, no flame or even smoke was ejected from the crater of the young volcano. Swinburne told me that he wrote the "Baudelaire" in a Turkish bath in Paris. (There were stranger groves of Academe than this.) No doubt the biographers of the future, intent on rubbing the gold-dust off the butterflies' wings, will tell us everything day by day. Meanwhile, these early years continue to be delightfully mysterious, and he was nearly thirty when he dawned in splendour on London.

Swinburne's second period lasted from 1865 to 1871. This was the blossoming-time of the aloe, when its acute perfume first filled the literary *salons*, and then emptied them; when for a very short time the poet emerged from his life-long privacy and trod the social stage. The experiment culminated, I suppose, in his solitary public utterance. He might be called "Single-speech Swinburne," since positively his only performance on his legs was an after-dinner oration, in May 1866, when he responded to the toast of "The Imaginative Literature of England" at Willis's Rooms. This second period was brilliant, but stormy. Swinburne was constitutionally unfitted to shine in mixed society. The events in his career now came fast and thick. The "Atalanta," acclaimed in 1865, had been followed later in the same year by "Chastelard," which made old men begin to dream dreams, and in 1866 by "Poems and Ballads," which roused a scandal unparalleled since Byron left England exactly half a century before.'

Then, when the fury of the public was at its height, there was a meeting between Jowett and Mazzini, at the house of Mr. George Howard (afterwards the ninth Earl of Carlisle), to discuss "what can be done *with* and *for* Algernon." And then there came the dedication to the Republic, "the beacon-bright Republic far-off sighted," and all the fervour and intellectual frenzies were successfully diverted from "such tendrils as the wild Loves wear" to the luminous phantasms of liberty and tyrannicide, to the stripping of the muffled souls of kings, and to all the other glorious, generous absurdities of the Mazzini-haunted "Songs before Sunrise" (1871). This was the period when, after an unlucky experience of London Society, the poet fled to the solitudes again, and nearly lost his life swimming in the harbour of Etretat. Of this episode I shall presently give a full account. The autumn of 1870 saw him once again in London. It is at this moment, when Swinburne was in his thirty-fourth year, that the recollections which I venture to set down before they be forgotten practically begin. They represent the emotional observations of a boy on whom this mysterious and almost symbolical luminary turned those full beams which were then and afterwards so thriftily withdrawn from the world at large.

That I may escape as quickly as possible from the necessity of speaking of myself, and yet may detail the credentials of my reminiscences, let me say that my earliest letter from Swinburne was dated September 14, 1867, when I was still in my eighteenth year, and that I first saw him in 1868. I was not presented to him, however, until the last week in 1870, when, in a note from the kind hostess who brought us together, I find it stated: "Algernon took to you at once, as is seldom the case with him." In spite of this happy beginning, the acquaintance remained superficial until 1873, when, I hardly know how, it ripened suddenly into an intimate friendship. From that time until he left London for good in the autumn of 1879 I saw Swinburne very frequently indeed, and for several years later than that our intercourse continued to be close. These relations were never interrupted, except by his increasing deafness and general disinclination to leave home. I would, then, say that the memories

I venture to bring forward deal mainly with the years from 1873 to 1880, but extend a little before and after that date.

I

The physical conditions which accompany and affect what we call genius are obscure, and have hitherto attracted little but empirical notice. It is impossible not to see that the absolutely normal man or woman, as we describe normality, is very rarely indeed an inventor, or a seer, or even a person of remarkable mental energy. The bulk of what are called entirely "healthy" people add nothing to the sum of human achievement, and it is not the average navvy who makes a Darwin, nor the typical daughter of the plough who develops into an Elizabeth Barrett Browning. There are probably few professional men who offer a more insidious attack upon all that in the past has made life variegated and interesting than the school of robust and old-fashioned physicians who theorise on eccentricity, on variations of the type, as necessarily evil and obviously to be stamped out, if possible, by the State. The more closely we study, with extremely slender resources of evidence, the lives of great men of imagination and action since the beginning of the world, the more clearly we ought to recognise that a reduction of all the types to one stolid uniformity of what is called "health" would have the effect of depriving humanity of precisely those individuals who have added most to the beauty and variety of human existence.

This question is one which must in the near future attract the close and sympathetic attention of the medical specialist. At present there seems to be an almost universal confusion between morbid aberration and wholesome abnormality. The presence of the latter amongst us is, indeed, scarcely recognised, and an unusual individuality is almost invariably treated as a subject either of disease or of affected oddity. When the physical conditions of men of the highest celebrity in the past are touched upon, it is usual to pass them over with indifference, or else to account for them as the results of disease. The peculiarities of Pascal, or of Pope, or of Michelangelo are either denied, or it is presumed that they were the result of purely morbid factors against which their genius, their rectitude, or their common-sense more or less successfully contended. It is admitted that Tasso had a hypersensitive constitution, which cruelty tortured into melancholia, but it is taken for granted that he would have been a greater poet if he had taken plenty of outdoor exercise. Descartes was of a different opinion, for though his body was regarded as feeble and somewhat abnormal, he considered it a machine well suited to his own purposes, and was convinced that the Cartesian philosophy would not have been improved, though the philosopher's digestion might, by his developing the thews of a ploughboy.

These reflections are natural in looking back upon

the constitution of Swinburne, which I believe to have been one of the most extraordinary that have been observed in our time. It would be a pity if its characteristics should be obscured by caricature on the one hand or by false sentiment on the other. In the days when I watched him closely I found myself constantly startled by the physical problem: What place has this singular being in the *genus homo?* It would easily be settled by the vague formula of "degeneration," but to a careful eye there was nothing in Swinburne of what is known as the debased or perverse type. The stigmata of the degenerate, such as we have been taught to note them, were entirely absent. Here were, to the outward and untechnical perception at least, no radical effects of disease, hereditary or acquired. He stood on a different physical footing from other men; he formed, as Cowley said of Pindar, "a vast species alone." If there had been a planet peopled by Swinburnes, he would have passed as an active, healthy, normal specimen of it. All that was extraordinary in him was not, apparently, the result of ill-health, but of individual and inborn peculiarity.

The world is familiar from portraits, and still better from caricatures, with his unique appearance. He was short, with sloping shoulders, from which rose a long and slender neck, surmounted by a very large head. The cranium seemed to be out of all proportion to the rest of the structure. His spine was rigid, and though he often bowed the heaviness of his head, *lasso papavera collo*, he seemed never to bend his back. Except in consequence of a certain physical weakness, which probably may, in more philosophical days, come to be accounted for and palliated—except when suffering from this external cause, he seemed immune from all the maladies that pursue mankind. He did not know fatigue; his agility and brightness were almost mechanical. I never heard him complain of a headache or of a toothache. He required very little sleep, and occasionally when I have parted from him in the evening after saying "Good-night," he has simply sat back in the deep sofa in his sitting-room, his little feet close together, his arms against his side, folded in his frock-coat like a grasshopper in its wing-covers, and fallen asleep, apparently for the night, before I could blow out the candles and steal forth from the door. I am speaking, of course, of early days; it was thus about 1875 that I closely observed him.

He was more a hypertrophied intelligence than a man. His vast brain seemed to weigh down and give solidity to a frame otherwise as light as thistledown, a body almost as immaterial as that of a fairy. In the streets he had the movements of a somnambulist, and often I have seen him passing like a ghost across the traffic of Holborn, or threading the pressure of carts eastward in Gray's Inn Road, without glancing to the left or the right, like something blown before a wind. At that time I held a humble post at the British Museum, from which I was freed at four o'clock, and Swinburne liked to arrange to meet me half-way between that monument and his own lodgings. One of Swinburne's peculiarities was an extreme punctuality, and we seldom failed to meet on the deserted northern pavement of Great Coram Street. But although the meeting was of his own making, and the person to be met a friend seen every day, if I stood a couple of yards before him silent, he would endeavour to escape on one side and then on the other, giving a great shout of satisfaction when at length his eyes focused on my face.

He was very fond of talking about his feats of swimming and riding as a boy, and no other poet has written about the former exercise with so much felicity and ardour:

> *As one that ere a June day rise*
> *Makes seaward for the dawn, and tries*
>   *The water with delighted limbs,*
>   *That tastes the sweet dark sea, and swims*
> *Right eastward under strengthening skies,*
>   *And sees the gradual rippling rims*
> *Of waves whence day breaks blossom-wise*
>   *Take fire ere light peer well above,*
>   *And laughs from all his heart with love;*
>
> *And softlier swimming, with raised head,*
> *Feels the full flower of morning shed,*
>   *And fluent sunrise round him rolled,*
>   *That laps and laves his body bold*
> *With fluctuant heaven in water's stead,*
>   *And urgent through the growing gold*
> *Strikes, and sees all the spray flash red,*

*And his soul takes the sun, and yearns
For joy wherewith the sea's heart burns.* . . .

There is nothing to approach it elsewhere in literature. It was founded on experience in the surf of Northumberland, and Swinburne's courage and zest as a bather were superb. But I was assured by earlier companions that he made remarkably little way by swimming, and that his feats were mainly of floating, his little body tossing on the breakers like a cork. His father, the admiral, had taught him to plunge in the sea when he was a very little child, taking him up in his arms and flinging him out among the waves. His cousin, Lord Redesdale, tells me that at Eton Algernon "could swim for ever," but he was always muscularly feeble, making up for this deficiency by his splendid courage and confidence.

No physiologist who studied the corporeal condition of Swinburne could avoid observing the violent elevation of spirits to which he was constantly subject. The slightest emotional excitement, of anger, or pleasure, or admiration, sent him into a state which could scarcely be called anything but convulsive. He was like that little geyser in Iceland which is always simmering, but which, if it is irritated by having pieces of turf thrown into it, instantly boils over and flings its menacing column at the sky. I was never able to persuade myself whether the extraordinary spasmodic action of the arms and legs which accompanied these paroxysms was the result of nature or habit. It was violent and it was long-continued, but I never saw that it produced fatigue. It gradually subsided into a graceful and smiling calm, sometimes even into somnolence, out of which, however, a provocative remark would instantly call up again the surprising spasm of the geyser. The poet's surviving sister, Miss Isabel Swinburne, tells me that this trick of stiffly drawing down his arms from the shoulders and giving a rapid vibratory movement to his hands was voluntary in childhood; she considers that it spoiled his shoulders and made them sloping. In later years I am sure it had become instinctive and unconscious. She describes to me also the extraordinary ecstasy which shook his body and lighted up his face when reading a book which delighted him or when speaking of any intellectual pleasure. Swinburne seemed to me to divide his hours between violent cerebral excitement and sheer immobility, mental and physical. He would sit for a long time together without stirring a limb, his eyes fixed in a sort of trance, and only his lips shifting and shivering a little, without a sound.

The conception of Swinburne, indeed, as incessantly flamboyant and convulsive is so common that it may be of value to note that he was, on the contrary, sometimes pathetically plaintive and distressed. The following impression, written down next day (January 4, 1878), reveals a Swinburne little imagined by the public, but frequently enough to be observed in those days by

Swinburne

intimate friends. It describes a slightly later condition than that on which I have hitherto dwelt:

"Swinburne has become very much at home with us, and, knowing our eating-times, he drops in every fortnight or so to dinner, and stays through the evening. All this winter he has been noticeably worn and feeble, sometimes tottering like an old man, and glad to accept a hand to help him up and down stairs. I hear he is very violent between whiles, but he generally visits us during the exhaustion and depression which follow his fits of excitement, when he is tired of his loneliness at Great James Street, and seems to crave the comfort of home-life and the petting that we lavish on him. Last night he arrived about 5 P.M.; he was waiting for me when I came back from the office. The maid had seen him into my study, brightened the fire and raised the lamp, but although she left him cosily seated under the light, I found him mournfully wandering, like a lost thing, on the staircase. We happened to be quite alone, and he stayed on for six hours. He was extremely gentle, bright, and sensible at dinner, full of gay talk about early memories, his recollections of Dickens, and odd anecdotes of older Oxford friends, Jowett, Stubbs, and the present Bishop of Ely [James Russell Woodford]. Directly dinner was over he insisted on seeing the baby, whom on these occasions he always kisses, and worships on his knees, and is very fantastic over. When he and I were alone, he closed up to the fire, his great head bowed, his knees held tight together, and his finger-tips pressed to his chest, in what I call his 'penitential' attitude, and he began a long tale, plaintive and rather vague, about his loneliness, the sadness of his life, the suffering he experiences from the slanders of others. He said that George Eliot was hounding on her myrmidons to his destruction. I made out that this referred to some attack in a newspaper which he supposes, very groundlessly I expect, to be inspired by George Eliot. Swinburne said that a little while ago he found his intellectual energy succumbing under a morbid distress at his isolation, and that he had been obliged steadily to review before his conscience his imaginative life in order to prevent himself from sinking into despair. This is only a mood, to be sure; but if there be any people who think so ill of him, I only wish they could see him as we see him at these recuperative intervals. Whatever he may be elsewhere, in our household not a kinder, simpler, or more affectionate creature could be desired as a visitor. The only fault we find with him is that his little mournful ways and his fragility drag painfully upon our sympathy."

This, it will be admitted, is not the Swinburne of legend in the seventies, and that it is so different may be judged, I hope, my excuse for recording it. A very sensible further change came over him when he was attacked by deafness, an infirmity to which, I believe, most members of his family have been liable. I do not think that I noticed any hardness of hearing until 1880, when the affliction rapidly developed. He was, naturally, very much concerned at it, and in the summer of that year he wrote to a lady of my household, "If this gets worse I shall become wholly unfit to mix in any society where two or three are gathered together." It did get worse; it was constitutional and incurable, and for the last quarter of a century of his life he was almost impervious to outward sound. All the more, therefore, was he dependent on the care of the devoted friend who thenceforward guarded him so tenderly.

II

The year 1868 was one of the most troubled in Swinburne's existence. He had now reached his thirty-second year, and there had succeeded a reaction to his juvenile flow of animal spirits, to his inexhaustible fecundity, and even to the violent celebrity which had stimulated and incited him as with the sting of a gad-fly. His first period of creative energy had come to a close, and he had not yet begun, or only now was beginning to launch steadily upon, his second, namely, the celebration in transcendental verse, and under the auspices of Mazzini, of the ideal and indivisible Republic. He was dejected in mind and ailing in body; the wonderful colours of youth were now first beginning to fade out of his miraculous eyes and hair. In

April, having written "The Hymn of Man," and having sent his great prose monograph on "William Blake" to the press, Swinburne paused and looked round him with a melancholy which had never afflicted him before. He complained, humorously and angrily, of "illness hardly intermittent during weeks and months of weather which would have disgraced hell and raised a revolution among devils." His principal pleasure was the encouragement given him by Mazzini, "my beloved Chief, still with us, very ill and indomitable, and sad and kind as ever." "Siena" was finished in May, and "Tiresias" was begun in June. Swinburne was doggedly and painfully working at what he always called "*His* book," the Chief's book, the volume of political lyrics which Mazzini had commanded him to write for the glory of Liberty and Italia.

It was in the evening of July 10, 1868, that I first cast eyes on the poet who was at that time the divinity, the object of feverish worship, to every budding artist and faltering singer in England. The occasion was accidental, the circumstances painful; it is enough to say that the idol was revealed to the juvenile worshipper at a startling moment of physical suffering and distress, and that the impression was one of curious terror, never, even under happier auspices, to be wholly removed. I shall not lose that earliest, and entirely unanticipated, image of a languishing and pain-stricken Swinburne, like some odd conception of Aubrey Beardsley, a *Cupido crucifixus* on a chair of anguish. I recall it here because, although in truth he was not nearly so ill as he looked, this apparition explains to me the imperative necessity which his friends found in the summer of that year to get him away from London, away from England, and if so, whither, if not to his beloved France?

It was projected that, so soon as he was well enough to move, he should go over to Boulogne, where a Welsh friend, Mr. Powell of Nant-Eôs, was to receive him. But this was not found immediately possible; the poet's journey was delayed, partly by his own continued weakness, then by an illness of his mother, so that it was not until September that he joined Powell at Etretat. Of this, his preliminary stay there, little record seems to remain. It was already late for bathing, and the weather turned bad. The party soon broke up. But Swinburne stayed long enough to form a great liking for the village, which was anything but the fashionable watering-place which it has since grown to be. It was a cluster of little old houses, with whitewashed walls and turfed roofs, inhabited by a sturdy race of Norman fishermen. Etretat had been "discovered" about ten years before this time by certain artists, particularly by Isabey and by the younger Clarkson Stanfield, all of whom kept their "discovery" very quiet. But Alphonse Karr, in his novels, had been unable to preserve a like reticence, and Paris had now waked up to the picturesque capacities of Etretat. Villas were beginning to be built along the edge of the two chalk cliffs and down the Grand Val.

It was none of these little smart villas, it was a dwelling of the local Norman type, which was to be identified in such a curious way with the legend of Swinburne.

Whether the purchase had already been made, or whether it was concluded after Swinburne left, or whether indeed the little place was not simply rented, year after year—at all events the beautified cottage in question passed about this time into the possession of Powell, who lived there for several years and entertained Swinburne summer after summer. He became an astonishing figure of eccentricity in the eyes of the simple fishermen of Etretat. It was he or Swinburne, or the precious pair of *farceurs* together, who gave the little house the sinister name of the Chaumière de Dolmancé, which presupposed a considerable amount of out-of-the-way reading in the passer-by who was to be scandalised. It did not scandalise, but very much "intrigued" a sturdy youth who often crossed its painted legend in his holidays, and who had already read enough "undesirable" literature to wonder what this was all about, and what odd beings chose to advertise that they inhabited the Chaumière de Dolmancé. It is necessary to sweep away a good many cobwebs of romance in dealing with the relations between Swinburne and Guy de Maupassant; for the sturdy youth was no other than he. In the following pages I hope to clear up, in some measure, the mystification which each of them wove around the legend in later years.

In the first place, it is needful to understand that Maupassant was not the famous writer he afterwards became. He was a youth of eighteen, and six years were to elapse before his nostrils snuffed up the odour of printers' ink. Etretat was his mother's summer home. Very soon after his birth Madame de Maupassant bought a small property in the Norman village, and here the future novelist's childhood was passed. The *curé* of Etretat prepared him for school, first for the seminary of the neighbouring town of Yvetot, that "citadel of Norman wit," and afterwards for Rouen; but all his holidays were spent among the fishermen of Etretat, going out with them in their boats by day and night, wrestling and climbing with their boys, scaling the slippery chalk cliffs to watch for their returning sails. It was not, therefore, a scandal-mongering journalist of Paris who pushed himself on the notice of the two Englishmen, but an extremely vivid and observant boy practically native to the soil, who examined the strange visitors with a wholly legitimate curiosity. The good faith of Guy de Maupassant, which has been called in question, must be defended. During these years, and till the war broke out, Maupassant was a student at the Lycée of Rouen, working under the benevolent eye of Gustave Flaubert, rapidly advancing in solid physical vigour, but giving little indication of his future line of action except in the painful writing of verses. He was, however, preternaturally wide-awake; and sweeping the horizon of Etretat, he became aware, summer after summer, of a remarkable pair of exotics.

The incident which led to his forming Swinburne's acquaintance must now be told with some minuteness, partly because, as an adventure, it was the most important in the poet's career, and partly because it has been made the subject of many vague and contradictory rumours. Swinburne, as we have already seen, was a daring bather, and one of the main attractions of Etretat was the facility it gave for exercise in the sea. On a certain Friday in the late summer at about 10 A.M., the poet went down alone to a solitary point on the eastern side of the *plage*, the Porte d'Amont—for there is no real harbour at Etretat—divested himself of his clothes, and plunged in, as was his wont. The next thing that happened was that a man called Coquerel, who was on the outlook at the semaphore, being at the foot of the cliffs on the eastern side of the bay, heard continued cries for help and piercing screams. He climbed up on a sort of rock of chalk, called Le Banc à Cuve, and perceived that a swimmer, who had been caught by the tide, which runs very heavily at that place, was being hurried out to sea, in spite of the violent efforts which he was making to struggle for his life. As it was impossible for Coquerel to do anything else to help the drowning man, he was starting to race along the shore to Etretat, when he saw coming round the point one of the fishing-smacks of the village. Coquerel attracted the attention of this boat, and directed the captain to the point out at sea where Swinburne's cries were growing fainter and further. The captain of the smack very cleverly seized the situation, and followed the poet, who had now ceased to struggle, but who supported himself by floating on the surface of the tide. This was hurrying him along so swiftly that he was not picked up until at a point a mile to the east-north-east of the eastern point of Etretat. It is a great pleasure to me, after more than forty years, to be able to give the name of the man who saved the life of one of the greatest poets of England. I hope that Captain Théodule Vallin may be remembered with gratitude by the lovers of literature.

The story hitherto is from Etretat sources. I now take it up as Swinburne told it to me, not very long after the event. His account did not differ in any essential degree from what has just been said. But he told me that soon after having left the Porte d'Amont he felt the under-current of the tide take possession of him, and he was carried out to sea through a rocky archway. Now, when it was too late, he recollected that the fishermen had warned him that he ought not to bathe without taking the tide into consideration. He tried to turn, to get out of the stream; but it was absolutely impossible, he was drawn on like a leaf. (What he did not say, of course, was that although he was absolutely untiring in the sea, and as familiar with it as a South Sea islander, the weakness of his arms prevented his being able to swim fast or far, so that he depended on frequent interludes of floating.) At first he fought to get out of the tide, and then, realising the hopelessness of this, he set himself to shout and yell, and he told me that the sound of his own voice, in that stillness of racing water, struck him as very strange and dreadful. Then he ceased to scream, and floated as limply as possible, carried along, and then he was suddenly aware that in a few minutes he would be dead, for the possibility of his being saved did not occur to him.

I asked him what he thought about in that dreadful contingency, and he replied that he had no experience of what people often profess to witness, the concentrated panorama of past life hurrying across the memory. He did not reflect on the past at all. He was filled with annoyance that he had not finished his "Songs before Sunrise," and then with satisfaction that so much of it was ready for the press, and that Mazzini would be pleased with him. And then he continued: "I reflected with resignation that I was exactly the same age as Shelley was when he was drowned." (This, however, was not the case; Swinburne had reached that age in March 1867; but this was part of a curious delusion of Swinburne's that he was younger by two or three years than his real age.) Then, when he began to be, I suppose, a little benumbed by the water, his thoughts fixed on the clothes he had left on the beach, and he worried his clouding brain about some unfinished verses in the pocket of his coat. I suppose that he then fainted, for he could not recollect being reached by the smack or lifted on board.

The fishermen, however, drew the poet successfully out of the water. Ivy should have grown up the masts and the sound of flutes have been heard in the forecastle, as when Dionysus boarded the pirate-vessel off Naxos. Captain Vallin was not much less astonished at his capture than the Icarians were, for Swinburne immediately displayed his usual vivacity. The *Marie-Marthe*—for that was the name of the boat—proceeded on her voyage to Yport. The weather was glorious; the poet's body was rubbed by the horny hands of his rescuers, and then wrapped in a spare sail, over which his mane of orange-ruddy hair was spread to dry, like a fan. He proceeded to preach to the captain and his men, who surrounded him, he told me, in rapturous approval, the doctrines of the Republic, and then he recited to them, "by the hour together," the poems of Victor Hugo. He was given some food, and in the course of the morning the *Marie-Marthe*, with her singular lading, tacked into the harbour of Yport.

Meanwhile, Swinburne's English friend and host, who had been near him on the shore, but not himself bathing, had, with gathering anxiety, seen him rapidly and unresistingly hurried out to sea through the rocky archway until he passed entirely out of sight. He immediately recollected—what Swinburne had forgotten—the treacherous under-currents so prevalent and so much dreaded on that dangerous coast. After Mr. Powell had lost sight of the poet for what seemed to him at least ten minutes, his anxiety was turned into horror, for there were shouts heard on the cliffs above him to the effect that "a man was drowning." He gathered up Swinburne's clothes in his arms, and ran ankle-deep in the loose shingle to where some boats were lying on the beach. These immediately started to the rescue; in but a few minutes after their departure, however, a boat arriving at Etretat from the east brought the welcome news that no catastrophe had happened, but that the *Marie-Marthe* had been seen to pick the Englishman up out of the water, and to continue her course towards Yport. Mr. Powell, therefore, took a carriage and galloped off at fullest speed, with Swinburne's clothes, and arrived at Yport just in time to see the *Marie-Marthe* enter the harbour, with Swinburne in excellent spirits and, wrapped in a sail, gesticulating on the deck.

What greatly astonished the Normans was that, after so alarming an adventure and so bitter an experience of the treachery of the sea, Swinburne was by no means willing to abandon it. The friends dismissed their carriage, and lunched at the pleasant little inn between the *place* and the sea; and having found that the *Marie-Marthe* was returning to Etretat in the afternoon, they took a walk along the cliffs until Captain Vallin had finished his business in Yport, when they returned with him by sea. This conduct was thought eccentric; it would have been natural to prefer a land journey at such a moment.

But, as the captain approvingly said, "C'eut été trop peu anglais." Everybody who had helped in the salvage was generously rewarded, and Swinburne and his friend were, for at least twenty-four hours, the most popular of the residents of Etretat.

It is not till now, at the twelfth hour, that Guy de Maupassant comes into the story. It is only fair to say that he never asserted, nor acquiesced in the assertion made by others, that he himself, on his own yacht, rescued Swinburne. A collegian of nineteen, at home for the holidays, a yacht was the last thing he was likely to possess. But he jumped on board one of those fishing-smacks which Mr. Powell sent out, and the boat he was on turned back only on hearing that the *Marie-Marthe* had already saved the drowning man. Who the latter was Maupassant did not learn until the evening of the same day, when he discovered that it was the English poet who had arrived, not long before, to be the guest of a strange Englishman, accomplished and extravagant, who occasionally conversed with Maupassant, as he paced the shingle-beach, and who had already excited his curiosity. "Ce Monsieur Powell," says Maupassant, "étonnait le pays par une vie extrêmement solitaire et bizarre aux yeux de bourgeois et de matelots peu accoutumés aux fantaisies et aux excentricités anglaises." In later years Maupassant was in the habit of describing, and doubtless of amplifying, for the amusement of Parisian friends, these "English eccentricities," and in particular he regaled Heredia and the Goncourts with them. Edmond de

Goncourt wrote a novel, once famous, which there are now none to praise and very few to read, called "La Faustin." This work is evidently founded on the gossip of Guy de Maupassant; but no one needs to waste his time searching in it for a portrait of Swinburne, for it is not there.

Maupassant's obliging zeal in hurrying to Swinburne's help was rewarded on the following day by an invitation to lunch at the Chaumière de Dolmancé. The two Englishmen were waiting for him in a pretty garden, verdurous and shady. Their visitor describes the house as "une toute basse maison normande construite en silex et coiffée de chaume," the very type of building in which the tragedies and comedies of rustic life in the Seine-Inférieure were to figure, years later, in the tales of the juvenile visitor. The eyes of that visitor, by the way, if youthful, were exceedingly sharp and bright; although he had not yet learned the artifice of prose expression, the power of observing and noting character was already highly developed in him. His account of the meeting, accordingly, is a very curious document, and one which a historian must touch with care. As it advances, with the desire to astonish and scandalise, it certainly borders on the apocryphal, and justifies Swinburne's indignation towards the end of his life. But the opening paragraphs bear the impress of absolute truth, and truth seen by the most clairvoyant of observers.

This, then, is how our poet struck the Norman boy who had never read a line of his verses. "M.

Swinburne was small and thin, amazingly thin at first sight, a sort of fantastic apparition. When I looked at him for the first time, I thought of Edgar Poe. The forehead was very large under long hair, and the face went narrowing down to a tiny chin, shaded by a thin tuft of beard. A very slight moustache slipped over lips which were extraordinarily delicate and were pressed together, while what seemed an endless neck joined this head, which was alive only in its bright, penetrating, and fixed eyes, to a body without shoulders, since the upper part of Swinburne's chest seemed scarcely broader than his forehead. The whole of this almost supernatural personage was stirred by nervous shudders. He was very cordial, very easy of access; and the extraordinary charm of his intelligence bewitched me from the first moment." There may be a touch of emphasis in this, a slight effect of caricature; but no one who knew Swinburne in those days will dare to deny the general fidelity of the portrait.

During the course of their life at Etretat the conversation of the friends continually turned on art, on literature, even on music, about which Powell was then greatly exercised. Swinburne did not recognise the difference between one tune and another, but he took a cerebral interest in music. The friends were entranced by the fame of Wagner and of Berlioz, who was much discussed in art circles; it is to be doubted whether either of them had heard any of the compositions of these musicians performed in public or in private. It was the attitude of Wagner which attracted and delighted them, while Swinburne had a curious conviction of sympathy with Berlioz, who died just about this time, leaving a mysterious reputation behind him. I have heard Swinburne express an overwhelming desire to be present when "La Damnation de Faust" was performed, and he was prepared, or almost prepared, to take a journey to Leipzig for that particular purpose. He had read some of Berlioz' musical criticism, which used to appear (I think) in *Le Figaro*, and he exulted in the French musician's eulogies of Shakespeare. The "Mémoires" of Berlioz were published later, but I think Swinburne had read "Les Grotesques de la Musique." Rapturous appreciation of music which he had never heard did not preclude, on Mr. Powell's part, enjoyment of music which he shared with all the world; and Offenbach, then laden with the laurels of "La Grande Duchesse de Gerolstein," was an honoured guest at the Chaumière while Swinburne was there.

But it was literature and art on which the poet discoursed with the greatest glow and abundance. Maupassant was dazzled, as well he might be, by the erudition, by the imagination, by the daring, by what seemed to him the perversity of the incredible English genius. It is impossible not to regret that Maupassant neglected, on the successive occasions when he spent some hours with Swinburne at Etretat, to note down, as he could have done, even at that early age, with admirable fidelity, some of the meteoric showers which crossed the vault of that high conversation. It is true that some of them, as the Frenchman merrily indicates, would demand, or would have demanded in mid-Victorian times, the gauze of Latinity to subdue their brilliance. Maupassant was particularly struck—and this is very interesting as the criticism of a Frenchman— with the Latin character of Swinburne's mind. He thought that the Roman imagination had no secrets from him, and Swinburne showed him Latin verses of his own, which Maupassant considered "admirables comme si l'âme de ce peuple [the Roman race] était restée en lui." Let us not ask whether the boy of eighteen was highly competent to judge of the Latinity of these verses; he could at least perfectly appreciate the poet's compliment.

As a Republican of the innermost sect of Mazzini it was necessary that Swinburne should proclaim, in season and out of season, his political convictions. He did not spare them to his young friend; and he did not conceal his loathing for "the Accursèd," as he called Napoleon III., then drawing much nearer to his end than anybody guessed. Maupassant was not scandalised by these opinions, but he noted the oddity of their being held by one so essentially an aristocrat, so much a noble to the tips of his fingers, as Swinburne evidently was. The visitor turned the subject to Victor Hugo, of whom the English poet spoke, as he always did, with unbridled enthusiasm. As Swinburne's flow of unaffected conversation became easier and fuller the astonishment of Maupassant increased. He thought his English acquaintance the most exasperatedly artistic human being whom he had ever met; and in later years, when he had become acquainted with all Paris, he still thought so. He was not altogether in sympathy with Swinburne, however. He considered that in his way of looking at literature and life there was something *macabre*; that, with all his splendour of thought, he suffered from a malady of spiritual vision, and that a perversity of temper mingled with the magic of his fancy. It would be folly to deny that, in this also, the young visitor showed a rare clairvoyance.

At the close of his visit to France in the summer of 1869 Swinburne devoted a month of the time otherwise spent at Etretat to an excursion of which no account has hitherto, I think, been published. It was in some ways so momentous, from the associations connected with it, that it ought to be recorded. Richard Burton, with whom Swinburne had now for some years been intimate, was appointed British consul in Damascus. As he had just returned from Santos in rather poor health, he was advised to take a course of the Vichy waters before he proceeded to Syria. He proposed that Swinburne should join him, which the poet, although greatly enjoying the sea-bathing at Etretat, instantly agreed to do. They met at Boulogne and reached Vichy on July 24. Five days later the poet wrote " Vichy suits me splendidly," and indeed he was now entering upon one of the most completely happy months of his life. He delighted in the breezy company of Burton, and at Vichy they found two other friends, Frederick Leighton and Adelaide Kemble (Mrs. Sartoris), whose "Week in a French Countryhouse" had recently revealed the existence of a new and exquisite humorist. This quartette of brilliant compatriots met daily, and entertained one another to the top of their bent. Many years afterwards, when the other three were dead, Swinburne celebrated this enchanting month at Vichy in a poem, called "Reminiscence," which he afterwards included in the "Channel Passage" volume under the title of "An Evening at Vichy." In it he describes

> *how bright the days [were] and how sweet their chime*
> *Rang, shone and passed in music that matched the clime*
> *Wherein we met rejoicing.*

He analyses of what the charm and what the radiance consisted, and he gives the first praise to

> *The loyal grace, the courtesy bright as day,*
> *The strong sweet radiant spirit of life and light*
> *That shone and smiled and lightened on all men's sight,*
> *The kindly life whose tune was the tune of May,*

in Leighton's conversation. Mrs. Sartoris was accustomed to sing for the three friends, with her incredible grace of vocalisation, and Swinburne describes how

c

A woman's voice, divine as a bird's by dawn
Kindled and stirred to sunward, arose and held
Our souls that heard, from earth as from sleep withdrawn,
And filled with light as stars, and as stars compelled
To move by might of music.

Finally, Burton's turn comes,

warrior and wanderer, crowned
With fame that shone from eastern or western day,
More strong, more kind, than praise or than grief might say.

It is surprising that this very important biographical poem has hitherto attracted so little attention from those who have written on the friendships of Swinburne. It was written in 1890.

While he was thus enjoying himself at Vichy, full of quiet happiness, he was lifted into the seventh heaven—"lit as a mountain lawn by morning," in his own words—through receiving a letter from Victor Hugo inviting him to stay with him at Hauteville House in Guernsey. Swinburne had sent the Master an article of his on the newly-published novel "L'Homme qui Rit." Victor Hugo wrote back "*such* a letter! thanking me *ex imo corde*, as he says (as if he to whom we all owe such thanks *could* have anything to thank any one for!), and ending up with 'Quand donc me sera-t-il donné de vous voir?'" Swinburne immediately and gratefully replied, "In a month's time, in September"; and on the same occasion he planned to spend "not more than a week" in Paris, on his way from Vichy to Guernsey. He made arrangements to meet in Paris Paul de Saint-Victor, Théophile Gautier, "and perhaps Gustave Flaubert." "Tu conviendras que cela veut bien la peine de s'arrêter ?" he writes at the close of July. But of all this glittering anticipation, nothing, I think, was realised. There was never a meeting with Gautier and Flaubert, and none with Hugo till it was too late for happiness. Why did the bright scheme fall through ? I do not know ; but when Sir Richard Burton went eastward to Damascus, it seems certain that Swinburne came dully back to Etretat, and he was in London in October. He possessed that winter an unpublished poem, "Les Enfants Pauvres," which Hugo had given him.

He wrote little during these summer holidays on the Norman coast. But it may be of interest to record that the magnificent "Epilogue" to "Songs before Sunrise," with its description of swimming at dawn, was composed at Etretat. The marvellous stanzas recording the sensations of the swimmer are a direct transcript of the ecstatic adventures in early morning hours from the *plage* outside the Porte d'Amont, or off the moorings of some indulgent and astonished fisherman. The poet's audacity in the waves was even sometimes alarming, as it had been twelve years before, when, as Miss Isabel Swinburne tells me, he insisted, in spite of the warning of the natives, upon plunging into the cold and dangerous waters of the Lac de Gaube, in the Pyrenees.

There remains only to add that the episode which

has been described on a previous page, in the course of which Swinburne so nearly lost his life, has left a direct mark on his poetry. It inspired "Ex-Voto," a poem written at Etretat, but not published until eight years later, when it was included in "Poems and Ballads, Second Series." I have the poet's own authority for stating this, and in particular for drawing attention to the fact that the following stanza (addressed, of course, to the sea) directly refers to his being nearly drowned:

> *When thy salt lips well-nigh*
> *Sucked in my mouth's last sigh,*
> *Grudged I so much to die*
>   *This death as others?*
> *Was it no ease to think*
> *The chalice from whose brink*
> *Fate gave me death to drink*
>   *Was thine—my Mother's?*

When the Franco-German War broke out, Swinburne was lingering at Etretat. He almost immediately returned to London, murmuring on the journey the strophes of an ode which he was already composing to the glory of a probable French Republic. He never, I believe, visited Etretat again.

III

The conversation of Swinburne, in the days of his youth and power, was very splendid in quality. No part of a great man disappears so completely as his table-talk, and of nothing is it more difficult afterwards to reconstruct an impression. Swinburne's conversation had, as was to be expected, some of the characteristics of his poetry. It was rapid, and yet not voluble; it was measured, ornate, and picturesque, and yet it was in a sense homely. It was much less stilted and involved than his prose writing. His extreme natural politeness was always apparent in his talk, unless, of course, some unfortunate *contretemps* should rouse a sudden ebullition, when he could be neither just nor kind. But, as a rule, his courtesy shone out of his blue-grey eyes and was lighted up by the halo of his cloud of orange hair as he waved it, gravely or waggishly, at the company. The ease with which finished and polished sentences flowed from him was a constant amazement to me I noted (January 1875) that somebody having been so unwise as to speak of the "laborious" versification of Catullus, Swinburne burst forth with a trumpet-note of scorn, and said, " Well, I can only tell you I should have called him the least laborious, and the most spontaneous, in his god-like and bird-like melody, of all the lyrists known to me except Sappho and Shelley; I should as soon call a lark's note 'laboured' as Catullus'." This might have been said of Swinburne's amazing talk; it was a stream of song, no more laboured than a lark's.

Immediately after leaving him I used sometimes, as well as I could, to note down a few of his sentences. It was not easy to retain much where all was so copious and rich, but a whole phrase or even colloquy would linger long in the memory. I think these brief reports may be trusted to give his exact words: nothing could recall his accent and the spontaneous *crescendo* effect of his enthusiasm. I quote from my note-books almost at random. This is in 1875, about some literary antagonist, but I have neglected to note whom:

"He had better be careful. If I am obliged" [very slowly] "to take the cudgel in my hand" [in rapid exultation] "the rafters of the hovel in which he skulks and sniggers shall ring with the loudest whacks ever administered in discipline or chastisement to a howling churl." All this poured forth, in towering high spirits, without a moment's pause to find a word.

Often Swinburne would put on the ironical stop, and, with a killing air of mock modesty, would say, "I don't know whether you can reasonably expect me to be *very* much weaker than a tame rabbit"; or "Even milk would boil over twice to be treated in that way."

He was certainly, during the years in which I knew him well, at his best in 1875. Many of the finest things which I tried to capture belonged to that year. Here is an instance of his proud humility:

"It is always a thorn in my flesh, and a check to any satisfaction which I might feel in writing prose, to reflect that probably I have never written, nor shall ever write, one single page that Landor would have deigned to sign. Nothing of this sort, or indeed of any sort whatever, troubles me for a moment when writing verse, but this always does haunt me when I am at work on prose."

Before 1875 he had become considerably severed from Rossetti in sympathy, and he was prepared to discuss without anger the possibility that his praise had been over-luscious :

"Well, very likely I did say some extravagant things about Rossetti's original sonnets and lyrics, but I do deliberately stick to any word I said about him as a translator. No doubt Shelley is to the full as beautiful a workman in that line, but then he is as inaccurate as Rossetti is accurate."

All through this year, 1875, his mind was full of the idea of translating Æschylus, Aristophanes, Villon, all his peculiar foreign favourites, and the subject was frequently uppermost in his mouth. He thought Mallarmé's version of Poe "very exquisite," although he could not make much of Manet's amazing folio illustrations. Swinburne was well disposed, however, to Manet, whose studio in Paris he told me he had visited in 1863, in company with Whistler and Fantin. He was much disappointed at the sudden death of Maggi, of Milan who had undertaken to bring out a complete Italian translation of his poems. Swinburne used to speak of Italy as "my second mother-country" and "my country by adoption," although I think his only personal knowledge of it had been gained in 1863, when he spent a long time in and near Florence, much of the time in the society of Walter Savage Landor and that "dear, brilliant, ingenious creature," Mrs. Gaskell. It was in a garden at Fiesole, he told me, that he wrote "Itylus," with the whole air vociferous with nightingales around him.

In the summer of 1875 I brought him a very laudatory review of his writings which had just appeared in Copenhagen, and urged him to gratify the Danish critic by sending him a few written words of acknowledgment. This he was very well pleased to do, but he paused, with lifted pen, and looking up sideways with that curious roguish smile which was one of his charms, he asked, "But what in the name of all the gods and little fishes of Scandinavia am I to say? I know! I must borrow some of the divine daring which enables our Master to respond so frankly to tributes of which he cannot read a word! I will write to your Danish friend exactly as Victor Hugo replies to such tributes of English verse and prose!"

The first letter, he told me, which he received from Victor Hugo, of whom he always spoke in terms of idolatrous reverence, was dated in the early part of 1862, in acknowledgment of some unsigned articles on "Les Misérables." In replying, with the greatest effusion, Swinburne asked leave to lay the dedication of "Chastelard" at Hugo's feet. Although the English poet always spoke of the French poet as a daughter might speak of her mother, with tender adoration, they did not meet until November 1882, when Swinburne went over to Paris on purpose to

Swinburne

attend the revival—"the resurrection," he called it—of "Le Roi s'amuse." He had no familiarity with Paris; he stayed, like a true British tourist, in one of the fashionable hotels in the Rue St. Honoré. On that occasion, and I think for the only time in his life, he pressed the hand of Victor Hugo. He wrote to me from Paris of the play, and of the fiftieth anniversary of its appearance, "a thing as unique and wonderful as the play itself," but said not a word of his impressions of Hugo.

To some one who remarked that it was disagreeable to be controverted, Swinburne replied gravely, "No! not at all! It gives a zest to the expression of sympathy to raise some points of amicable disagreement." This was not the only case in which I was struck by a certain unconscious resemblance between his repartees and those of Dr. Johnson.

Early in life he started his theory of the division of great writers into gods and giants. He worked it out rather whimsically; Shakespeare, of course, was a god, and Ben Jonson was a giant, but I think that Webster was a god. These conjectures led him along the pleasant pathway of caprice. He now started his serious study of Shakespeare, of which, as about to become a book, I believe he first spoke to me late in 1873. It was a time of controversy so acrid that we can hardly realise the bitterness of it in these calm days. But Swinburne was more than ready for the fight. He rejoiced in his power to make his assailants ridiculous. "I need hardly tell you," he said to me, "that I shall begin, and clear my way, with a massacre of the pedants worthy of one of Topsy's [William Morris's] Icelandic sagas. It shall be 'a murder grim and great,' I pledge myself to you!" And indeed he was very vivacious at the expense of the New Shakspere (or "Shack-spur," as he always pronounced it) Society.

Great anger burned in his bosom because the *Athenæum* described his "Erechtheus" as "a translation from Euripides." I never clearly understood the reason of Swinburne's fanatical objection to Euripides, which has even puzzled Dr. Verrall. He must have adopted it, I think, from Jowett. On the occasion of the appearance of the review quoted above, I found Swinburne in a fine fit of the tantrums. He poured out his indignation the moment I came into the room. "Translation from Euripides, indeed! Why, a fourth-form boy could perceive that, as far as "Erechtheus" can be said to be formed after anybody it is modelled throughout on the earlier style of Æschylus, the simple three-parts-epic style of 'The Suppliants,' 'The Persians,' and the 'Seven against Thebes,' the style most radically contrary to the 'droppings,' grrh! the *droppings* (as our divine and dearest Mrs. Browning so aptly rather than delicately puts it) of the scenic sophist that can be conceived. I should very much like to see the play of Euripides which contains five hundred consecutive lines that could be set against as many of mine!"

Again, on a later occasion, "I always have maintained, and I always shall maintain, that it is infinitely easier to overtop Euripides by the head and shoulders than to come up to the waist of Sophocles or stretch up to touch the lance of Æschylus." "Erechtheus" was written with unusual celerity, all of it, if I remember right, in lodgings by the sea at Wragford, near Southwold, in Suffolk, where Swinburne was staying in the autumn of 1875. When we think of the learning, the weight of imagination, and the unrivalled metrical daring of that splendid drama (to my mind on the very highest level of Swinburne's poetical achievement), this improvisation seems marvellous.

To one who praised in his presence the two great naval odes of Campbell : " I like to hear you say that. But I should speak still more passionately, for the simple fact is that I know nothing like them at all, *simile aut secundum*, in their own line, which is one of the very highest lines in the highest range of poetry. Very little national verse anywhere is good either patriotically or poetically; and what is good patriotically is far inferior to Campbell poetically. Look at Burns and Rouget de l'Isle! What is virtually lacking is proof, in the face of the Philistines, that poetry has real worth and weight in national matters—lacking everywhere else, only— *not* lacking in Campbell."

His feeling about literature was serious to the verge of fanaticism. It absorbed him like a religion, and it was this unflagging sense of the superhuman power and value of poetry which made his conversation so stimulating, especially to a very young man whom he honoured with the untrammelled expression of his opinions. But he had a charming delicacy of toleration for the feelings of those whom he respected, even when he believed them to be tainted with error. Of an elder writer of some authority, to whom he was urged to reply on a point of criticism, he said, "No! If I wrote about what he has said, I could not hold myself in. I do not wish to be rude to ——. Now, I know that I should begin by trying to behave like a good boy, and before I knew what I was doing I should be smiting —— hip and thigh, and making him as the princes were who perished at Endor. I hope you remember what *they* became? Look it up, and you will find what becomes of poeticules when they decompose into criticasters! So, you see, I had better leave him alone."

Swinburne's pleasure in fighting was a very marked and a very amusing trait in his conversation. He liked, at brief intervals, to have something to worry between the teeth of his discourse. He would allow himself to be drawn off the scent by any red herring of criticism. This mock irascibility, as of a miniature Boythorn, always struck me as having been deliberately modelled on the behaviour of Walter Savage Landor. This impression was confirmed in rather a startling way by a phrase of Swinburne's own. He had been reading to me the MS. of his "George Chapman," and after the reading was over, and we had passed to other things, Swinburne said, " Did you notice just now some pages of rather Landorian character? Don't you think I was rather like the old lion, when he was using his teeth and claws, in my rending of the stage licensers and our crazy English censorial system?"

IV

The intellectual temperament of Swinburne is not to be apprehended unless we remember that he was in grain an aristocrat. On the father's side he was directly descended from a feudal Border family, which, as long ago as the reign of Edward II., had produced a man of mark in Sir Adam de Swinburne. The poet never forgot the ancestral castle of Swinburne, which had passed from his forbears two centuries ago, never the fierce feuds and rattling skirmishes under the hard Northumbrian sky. He talked with freedom and with manifest pleasure of these vague mediæval forefathers, of their bargaining and fighting with the Umfrevilles and the Fenwicks; of the unspeakable charm of their fastness at Capheaton, where so much of his own childhood was passed. But his interest in the Swinburnes seemed to be largely romantic and antiquarian. His connections on his mother's side were not less distinguished, nor were they less ancient, although the Ashburnhams were ennobled by William III., and their immediate founder had been a loyal groom of the bedchamber to Charles I. The poet's interest in their history, however, began at the point where Lady Jane

Ashburnham married Admiral Charles Swinburne in 1836, Algernon being born next year as their eldest son. He was not indisposed, however, in unemphatic retrospect, to recall the great houses of Ormonde, Anglesey, and Northumberland with which the blood of his mother brought him into direct connection. Probably a reminiscence of all this may occasionally be found to throw light on some otherwise cryptic lines in his poetry.

Of all his relatives, however, he spoke in those days most of two: his incomparable mother, invincible in tenderness and anxious care, and his somewhat formidable uncle, the fourth Earl. This nobleman was a book-collector of the fearless old fashion, who had formed, at a reckless cost, one of the noblest libraries in England. Lord Ashburnham did not welcome visitors to his bookshelves, but he made a special, perhaps a unique, exception in favour of his nephew. Some of Swinburne's happiest days were spent among the almost fabulous treasures of the great house near Battle, and he would return to London with dazzled eyes, babbling of illuminated breviaries and old MS. romances in Burgundian French. There can be no doubt that Lord Ashburnham was one of the very few persons, if he was not the only one, of whom his nephew stood in awe. If the poet was fractious, the peer could be tumultuous, and I have been told that nowhere was Algernon so primly on his "p's and q's" as at Ashburnham. But a real affectionate appreciation existed between the old bibliophile and the glowing young poet. When Lord Ashburnham died, over eighty, in 1878, it was with sorrow as well as respect that his nephew mourned him.

Outside poetry, and, in lesser measure, his family life, Swinburne's interests were curiously limited. He had no " small talk," and during the discussion of the common topics of the day his attention at once flagged and fell off, the glazed eye betraying that the mind was far away. For science he had no taste whatever, and his lack of musical ear was a byword among his acquaintances. I once witnessed a practical joke played upon him, which made me indignant at the time, but which now seems innocent enough, and not without interest. A lady, having taken the rest of the company into her confidence, told Swinburne that she would render on the piano a very ancient Florentine ritornello which had just been discovered. She then played "Three Blind Mice," and Swinburne was enchanted. He found that it reflected to perfection the cruel beauty of the Medicis—which perhaps it does. But this exemplifies the fact that all impressions with him were intellectual, and that an appeal to his imagination would gild the most common object with romance.

In the days I speak of, Swinburne lived in large, rather empty rooms on the first floor of an old house in Great James Street, which used to remind me of one of Dickens's London houses in "Great Expectations" or "Little Dorrit." But until the death of his father, who died at a great age in the early autumn of 1877, Swinburne always had a country home in Holmwood, near Henley-on-Thames. At Admiral Swinburne's death I think he stayed on with his mother at Holmwood till the end of that year. Such months on the banks of the Thames were always beneficial to his health, and he wrote there without interruption. I find a note (1875): "How exuberant S. always is when he comes back; it is partly pleasure at being in London again, and partly refreshment from his country captivity." Of his visits to the sea-coast of Norfolk and Suffolk others must speak, for I never had the pleasure of accompanying him.

When he came back from the country to town he was always particularly anxious to recite or read aloud his own poems. In doing this he often became very much excited, and even, in his overwhelming sense of the movement of the metre, would jump about the room in a manner somewhat embarrassing to the listener. His method of procedure was uniform. He would arrive at a friend's house with a breast-pocket obviously bulging with manuscript, but buttoned across his chest. After floating about the room and greeting his host and hostess with many little becks of the head, and affectionate smiles, and light wavings of the fingers, he would settle at last upright on a chair, or, by preference, on a sofa, and sit there in a state of rigid immobility, the toe of one foot pressed against the heel of the other. Then he would say, in an airy, detached way, as though speaking of some absent person, "I have brought with me my

'Thalassius' or my 'Wasted Garden' (or whatever it might happen to be), which I have just finished." Then he would be folded again in silence, looking at nothing. We then were to say, " Oh, do please read it to us! Will you?" Swinburne would promptly reply, " I had no intention in the world of boring you with it, but since you ask me——" and out would come the MS. I do not remember that there was ever any variation in this little ceremony, which sometimes preluded many hours of recitation and reading. His delivery, especially of his own poetry, was delightful as long as he sat quietly in his seat. His voice, which was of extraordinary beauty, " the pure Ashburnham voice," as his cousin explains to me, rose and fell monotonously, but with a flute-like note which was very agreeable, and the pulse of the rhythm was strongly yet delicately felt. I shall never forget the successive evenings on which he read "Bothwell" aloud in his lodgings, in particular one on which Edward Burne-Jones, Arthur O'Shaughnessy, P. B. Marston, and I sat with him at his round marble-topped table—lighted only by candles in two giant candlesticks of serpentine he had brought from the Lizard—and heard him read the magnificent second act of that tragedy. He surpassed himself in vigour and melody of utterance that night. But sometimes, in reading, he lost control of his emotions, the sound became a scream, and he would dance about the room, the paper fluttering from his finger-tips like a pennon in a gale of wind.

He was not, in my recollection, very ready to recite old published poems of his own, though always glad, and even imperiously anxious, to read new ones. Almost the only exception which I remember was in favour of "The Triumph of Time," a poem which Swinburne deliberately impressed upon me, and doubtless upon other friends as well, as being, in a very peculiar sense, a record of personal experience. It was always difficult to know where the frontier ran between hard fact and Swinburne's mind illuminated by a sweeping limelight of imagination. He had a real love of truth, but no certain recognition of fact. Unless, however, he curiously deceived himself, a set of very definite emotions and events is embalmed in "The Triumph of Time," of which I have more than once heard him chant fragments with extraordinary poignancy. On these occasions his voice took on strange and fife-like notes, extremely moving and disconcerting, since he was visibly moved himself. The sound of Swinburne wailing forth in his thrilling semitones such stanzas as that addressed to the Sea :

> *I shall sleep, and move with the moving ships,*
>   *Change as the winds change, veer in the tide;*
> *My lips will feast on the foam of thy lips,*
>   *I shall rise with thy rising, with thee subside;*
> *Sleep, and not know if she be, if she were,*
> *Filled full with life to the eyes and hair,*
> *As a rose is fulfilled to the roseleaf tips*
>   *With splendid summer and perfume and pride,*

is something which will not fade out of memory a long as life lasts; and, perhaps, most of all, in the recitation of the last four of the following very wonderful verses:

> *I shall go my ways, tread out my measure,*
>   *Fill the days of my daily breath*
> *With fugitive things not good to treasure,*
>   *Do as the world doth, say as it saith;*
> *But if we had loved each other—O sweet,*
> *Had you felt, lying under the palms of your feet,*
> *The heart of my heart, beating harder with pleasure*
>   *To feel you tread it to dust and death,*

Swinburne seemed to achieve, or to go far towards achieving, an entirely novel and original form of expression. His whole body shook with passion, his head hung on one side with the eyes uplifted, his tongue seemed burdened by the weight of the syllables, and in the concentrated emphasis of his slow utterance he achieved something like the real Delphic ecstasy, the transfiguration of the Pythia quivering on her tripod. It was surpassingly strange, but it was without a touch of conscious oddity or affectation. It was a case of poetic "possession," pure and simple.

V

Swinburne was a prodigious worker, and the bulk of his productions in prose and verse is the more surprising since the act of writing was extremely disagreeable to him, as, we may remember, it was to Wordsworth.

He should have been born an improvisatore. I brought him once a picture of the Swedish poet Bellmann, whose genius (a hundred years earlier) had a certain resemblance to his own. Bellmann was represented with a lute, improvising his verses in the open air. "Ah!" said Swinburne, "that is what I should like to do! I should like to stand on a promontory in Sark, in the full blaze of the sun, and shout my verses till all the gulls come fawning to my feet. That would be better than scraping and spluttering over a filthy pen." In spite of a real physical difficulty in writing, however, Swinburne got through an astonishing amount. In the autumn of 1874, for instance, I find he was finishing "Bothwell"; he was preparing a volume of essays for the press; he was composing lyrics for a volume to be called "Songs in Time of Change," and then "Poems of Revolution" (ultimately, I suppose, "Songs of Two Nations"); he was writing criticism of Poe and Blake (which did not, I think, please him enough to be printed); he was busy with a book about Chapman; and he was engaged on a revival of Wells's "Joseph and His Brethren." In connection with the last-mentioned, I remember his showing me the recast he was making of an essay on Wells he had written in 1861, and he said, "At all events, I can write better prose now than I could then."

The habit of centenaries had not seized the British public forty years ago. The anniversary of Landor's birth passed quite unobserved, and even Swinburne did not recollect the date till the day itself, when he was at Holmwood, and could do nothing. He was extremely vexed; oddly enough, he had always believed Landor to be two or three years older than he was, and he had taken for granted that the centenary had passed. However, it providentially transpired that Charles Lamb was born only eleven days later than Landor, so on February 1, 1875, Swinburne came up to town, with delightful fussiness, on purpose to organise a Lamb dinner. So far as I know, it was the only time in his life that he ever "organised" anything. He was magnificent; very grave and important; and he smoothed over the awkward circumstance of his having forgotten (for the moment) his own beloved Landor by saying that the same libations might fitly and gracefully be mingled in an affectionate remembrance of the two great men.

Landor, however, was ultimately merged in Lamb, in whose honour a very small group ate a mediocre dinner in a Soho tavern on February 10. We were only five, if I recollect rightly, the others being Mr. Theodore Watts, our ardent and sanguine William Minto (whose bright life burned out untimely some nineteen years ago), and a curious friend of Swinburne's, Thomas Purnell, always to me rather a disturbing element. Swinburne was in the chair, and I never saw him in better "form." He took upon himself an air of dignity which presupposed the idea that our little banquet was, symbolically, a large public affair; and when Purnell "went too far," as people say, it was wonderful to hear

Swinburne recall him to a more decorous choice of language. I feel as if there had been "speeches"; but that is merely caused by a recollection of the very high grade along which the conversation moved until the waiters turned us out into the street.

Of the relations between Swinburne and Browning something should, I believe, be put on record. In the earliest times the former had shared the Pre-Raphaelite enthusiasm for what Browning had published up to "Men and Women." But the two poets came into no close contact, and I think that Swinburne's natural instinct was not attracted to Browning's personality. When, in 1874, I began eagerly to talk of the elder to the younger poet, my zeal was checked by Swinburne's courteous indifference. He found no pleasure whatever in Browning's plays, nor much, which astonished me, in his lyrics. Yet there was no aversion, and when we came to "The Ring and the Book" Swinburne's praise was unaffected. Moreover, he more and more warmly admired the series of psychological studies beginning with "Fifine at the Fair." "This," he said, "is far better than anything Browning has yet written. Here is his true province." The result of this development of taste was the page of almost extravagant laudation in the "George Chapman" of 1875, which amazed some of Swinburne's friends, and bewildered Browning himself as much as it gratified him. But, unfortunately, in 1877, at the height of Swinburne's violent controversy with the New Shakspere Society, Browning accepted the presidency of that body. This gave Swinburne not merely deep offence, but great and lasting pain, and no invectives became too sharp for him in speaking of Browning. It distressed me beyond measure that such a misunderstanding should exist between men whom I loved and venerated, and I ventured to tell Browning how much Swinburne was hurt. He was, of course, entirely innocent of all intentional offence, expressed himself shocked, and begged me to explain to Swinburne how little any intention of slighting him had crossed his mind. At the same time, for my private ear, Browning suggested that one's conduct really could not be regulated by the dread lest some eminent person one scarcely knew might disapprove of it. I did what I could, not without some success, to moderate Swinburne's anger, but the damage was done. There was a native incompatibility between the two poets which prevented either of them from according complete justice to the other. The character of Browning had the breadth of a lake, which is sometimes swept by storms; that of Swinburne, the unceasing impetuosity of a mountain torrent.

Before his fortieth year there had set in a curious ossification of Swinburne's intellect. He ceased to form new impressions, while reverting with all his former exuberance to the old. This was extraordinary in one who had waved the banner of rebellion and had led youthful enthusiasm so heroically when it affected writers just earlier than himself. Whether he changed his tone in familiar talk later on I do not know, but certainly between 1874 and 1884 he showed no intelligent comprehension whatever of the new elements in literature. He was absolutely indifferent to Stevenson, to Ibsen, to Dostoieffsky, each of whom was pressed upon his notice, and his hostility to Zola was grotesque. In 1877 "L'Assommoir" was published periodically in a Paris review called, I think, *La République des Lettres*, a journal which had languished from the first, and now expired in its third volume. Swinburne attributed, of course jocosely, the fact of its failure to the effect of a most dignified protest against Zola which he had printed somewhere. I remember his ecstasy, and his expression of a belief (which proved quite unfounded) that Zola would never dare to publish another page.

This attitude to the French Naturalists was unusual. Swinburne's native temper was generous, and the idea of attacking a genuine talent of any species would have been dreadful to him. But he did not think that Stevenson—to take a particularly distressing instance—had any talent, and he was therefore silent about what he wrote. It was curious, however, to note that Swinburne was always capable of being affected along straight lines of reminiscence. At the very moment when he was hewing at the French realists, root and branch, he spoke to me with generous approval of one of the least gifted and most extreme of their precursors, Léon Cladel. I was greatly astonished, but the mystery was soon explained. Cladel had attacked Napoleon III. with peculiar virulence, and he was an open worshipper at the altar of Victor Hugo. No matter how Zolaesque his stories might be, he had these two unquestionable claims on Swinburne's approbation.

There is no doubt that a wonderful aura of charm hung about the person of this astonishing man of genius. Swinburne might be absurd; he could not fail to be distinguished. He might be quixotic; he was never mean or timid or dull. He represented, in its most flamboyant shape, revolt against the concessions and the hypocrisies of the mid-Victorian era, " this ghastly, thin-faced time of ours." An extraordinary exhilaration accompanied his presence, something uplifted, extravagant, and yet unselfish. No one has ever lived who loved poetry more passionately, found in it more inexhaustible sources of pleasure, cultivated it more thoroughly for itself, more sincerely for nothing which it might be persuaded to offer as a side issue. Half Swinburne's literary influence depended upon little, unregarded matters, such as his unflinching attitude of worship towards the great masters, his devotion to unpopular causes, his uncompromising arrogance in the face of conventionality. It is becoming difficult to recapture even the thrill he caused by his magic use of "unpoetic" monosyllables, such as "bloat," "pinch," "rind," "fang," "wince," embedded in the very heart of his ornate melody. But his meteoric flight across the literary heavens, followed by the slow and dignified descent of the glimmering shower of sparks, will long excite curiosity, even when the sensation it caused has ceased to be quite intelligible. Yet those who stood under the apparition, and stared in amazement at its magnificent audacity, must not be over-much surprised if a generation is arising that fails to comprehend what the phenomenon meant to the original spectators.

1909–12.

PHILIP JAMES BAILEY
1816–1902

PHILIP JAMES BAILEY

AT the opening of the year 1902 there were still alive amongst us two men who survived as representatives of what poetry was in these islands before the commencement of the Victorian era. Mr. Aubrey de Vere, having reached his eighty-ninth year, passed away on January 20; Mr. Philip James Bailey, in his eighty-seventh, on September 7. So, as we sit quietly and watch, we see history unrolling, since, in the chronicle of our literature, the closure of a great and complicated system of poetic activity was, in a sense, defined by the deaths of these venerable men. Moreover—and this is curious—in each of these survivors we had, living before us, types—not quite of the first order, indeed, but yet vivid types—of the two main divisions of the English poetry of the first half of the nineteenth century: that, namely, which was devoted to a reasonable grace, and that which was uplifted on a mystical enthusiasm. So that a sermon on the verse of that time might well take as its text the opposed and yet related names of De Vere and Bailey.

Nothing so extensive is to be attempted here. But before endeavouring to define the character of the talent of the younger of these veterans, and to note the place of "Festus" in the history of letters, we may linger a moment on what resemblance there was between the two aged men, so intensely opposed in their general disposition of mind and their walk in the world. They had in common an exquisite personal dignity, Mr. de Vere moving in the genial companionship of like-minded friends, both in Ireland and in London; Mr. Bailey immobile in his hermitage at Nottingham. They had in common the happy fate which preserved to each in extreme old age all the faculties of the mind, the sweetest cheerfulness, the most ardent hopefulness, an optimism that nothing could assail and that disease itself avoided. Each, above all, to a very remarkable degree, preserved to the last his religious devotion to that art to which his life had been dedicated; each to the very end was full of a passionate love of verse. Song-intoxicated men they were, both of them; preserving their delight in poetry far beyond the common limits of an exhilaration in any mental matter.

When this has been said, it is the difference far more than the resemblance between them which must strike the memory. Of the imaginative opposition which the author of "Festus" offered to the entire school of which Mr. de Vere was a secondary ornament more will be said later. But the physical opposition was immense between the slightness of figure and flexible elegance of the

Irish poet, with his mundane mobility, and the stateliness of Mr. Bailey. Mr. de Vere never seemed to be an old man, but a young man dried up; Mr. Bailey, of whose appearance my recollections go back at least thirty years, always during that time looked robustly aged, a sort of prophet or bard, with a cloud of voluminous white hair and curled silver beard. As the years went by his head seemed merely to grow more handsome, almost absurdly, almost irritatingly so, like a picture of Connal, "first of mortal men," in some illustrated edition of Ossian. The extraordinary suspension of his gaze, his gentle, dazzling aspect of uninterrupted meditation, combined with a curious downward arching of the lips, seen through the white rivers of his beard, to give a distinctly vatic impression. He had an attitude of arrested inspiration, as if waiting for the heavenly spark to fall again, as it had descended from 1836 to 1839, and as it seemed never inclined to descend again. But the beauty of Mr. Bailey's presence, which was so marked as to be an element that cannot be overlooked in a survey of what he was, had an imperfection in its very perfectness. It lacked fire. What the faces of Milton and Keats possessed, what we remember in the extraordinary features of Tennyson, just this was missing in Mr. Bailey, who, nevertheless, might have sat to any scene-painter in Christendom as the type of a Poet.

I

English literature in the reign of William IV. is a subject which has hitherto failed to attract a historian. It forms a small belt or streak of the most colourless, drawn across our variegated intellectual chronicle. The romantic movement of the end of the preceding century had gradually faded into emotional apathy by 1830, and the years which England spent under the most undignified and inefficient of her monarchs were few indeed, but highly prosaic. Most of the mental energy of the time went out in a constitutional struggle which was necessary, but was not splendid. A man is hardly at his best when his own street-door has been slammed in his face, and he stands outside stamping his feet and pulling the bell. The decade which preceded the accession of Victoria was, in literature, a period of cold reason : the best that could be said of the popular authors was that they were sensible. A curious complacency marked the age, a self-sufficiency which expressed itself in extraordinarily unemotional writing. To appreciate the heavy and verbose deadness of average English prose in the thirties we must dip into the books then popular. No volume of the essay class was so much in vogue as the "Lacon" of the Rev. Mr. Colton, a work the aridity of which can only be comprehended by those who at this date have the courage to attack it. Mr. Colton, although he preached the loftiest morality, was a gambling parson, and shot himself, in 1832, in the Forest of Fontainebleau. But that did not affect the popularity of his chain of dusty apophthegms.

The starvation of the higher faculties of the mind in the William IV. period was something which we fail to-day to realise. No wonder Carlyle thought, in 1835, that "Providence warns me to have done with literature," and in 1837 saw nothing for it but to "buy a rifle and a spade, and withdraw to the Transatlantic wilderness." In the letters of Tennyson we may easily read what it was that, after the failure of his enchanting volumes of 1830 and 1833, kept him silent in despair for ten of his best years. This was the dead lull during which the moral storms of 1840-1850 were preparing to gather. It was the time when the Puseyite controversy was beginning, when "Tracts for the Times," under an oppressive obloquy and miscomprehension, were making a struggle for religious warmth and air. A chilly light of reason applied to morals, that was what the subjects of William IV. desired to contemplate, and poetry itself was called upon to make a definite concession to the gospel of utility. Romance was at its lowest ebb, and even—

*the ghost of Miltiades rose by night
And stood by the bed of the Benthamite.*

Among poets who possessed the public ear at that time, the aged Wordsworth stood first, but the prestige of the laureate, Southey, who had been one of the most active and authoritative of reviewers,

E

was, in many circles, paramount. Now Southey—as his most prominent disciple, Sir Henry Taylor, has proudly told us—"took no pleasure in poetic passion." By the time of which we are speaking, however, Southey and even Wordsworth had passed into the background of active life, but there had been no reaction against the quietism of their later days. That quietism had taken possession of the taste of the country, and had gradually ousted the only serious rival it had seemed to possess, the violence of Byron. It was at this time, in the full tide of Benthamism, that Henry Taylor attempted a poetical *coup d'état* which demands close attention from the student of our literary history.

In publishing his enormous drama of "Philip van Artevelde," in 1834, Henry Taylor took occasion to issue a preface which is now far more interesting to read than his graceful verse. He thought the time had come to stamp out what he called "the mere luxuries of poetry." He was greatly encouraged by the general taste of the public, which obviously was finding highly-coloured literature inacceptable, and in a preface of singular boldness, not unadroit in its logic, Taylor presumed to dictate terms to the poets. He begged them, for the future, to walk the common earth and breathe the common air. He entreated them to believe that forcible expression, fervid feeling, and beautiful imagery are useless if employed in connection with thoughts that are not "sound." There was to be no health for us unless reason had full supremacy over imagination.

Reflection must take the place of mere "feeling," thought the place of imagery. Passion, so this faithful disciple of Southey thought, was to be regarded as a direct danger and disadvantage.

Nor did the preface of 1834 confine itself to the encouragement of what was tame and good; it descended into the dust, and wrestled with lions that were wild and bad. It fought with Byron, as Christian fought with Apollyon, conscious of the awful strength of its supernatural opponent. It fought less strenuously, and with a touch of contempt, with "the brilliant Mr. Shelley," to whom it could afford to be condescending. It glanced round the arena without being able so much as to observe an antagonist who, to our eyes, fills the picture, and is alone sufficient to condemn all the "Philip van Artevelde" arguments and theories. This is Keats, of whom, so far as we can discover from this preface, Taylor had, in 1834, never even heard, or else despised so entirely that it did not occur to him to mention his name.

The Preface to "Philip van Artevelde" enjoyed a great success. Its assumptions were accepted by the reviewers as poetic canon law. It was admitted without reserve that the function of poetry was "to infer and to instruct." The poets were warned to occupy themselves in future mainly with what was rational and plain. Henry Taylor had made the sweeping charge that the more enthusiastic species of verse was apt to encourage attention by fixing it on what is "puerile, pusillanimous, or wicked." There was a great searching of heart in families; the newspapers were immense. A large number of copies of "Childe Harold" and of "Manfred" were confiscated, and examples of Pollok's "Course of Time" (by many persons preferred to "Paradise Lost," as of a purer orthodoxy) were substituted for them. Even the young Macaulay, who had suddenly become a power, joined the enemy, and declared that "perhaps no person can be a poet, or can ever enjoy poetry, without a certain unsoundness of mind." Ah, but, cries in effect the excellent Henry Taylor, we will so coerce and browbeat and depress the poets that they shall not think a thought or write a line that is not "sound," and the Benthamite himself (the stupendous original Jeremy had died, of course, in 1832) shall pluck, unhandily enough, at the lyre now consecrated to utility and decorum.

It was the old balance between "stasy" and "ec-stasy," and Henry Taylor was, to a certain extent, justified by the character of such contemporary works as might be held to belong to the ecstatic species. It did not seem a moment at which great subjects and a great style were prepared to commend themselves. The most prominent indulgers in "the mere luxury of poetry" were Heraud and Reade, whose efforts were calculated to bring instant ridicule upon imaginative writing by their hollow grandiloquence. There were the Byronisms of Croly, the once-famous author of that gorgeous romance, "Salathiel," and there was the never-to-be-forgotten Robert Montgomery. All these poetasters merely emphasised and justified Henry Taylor's protest. In genuine poetry of a highly imaginative cast there appeared, almost wholly unregarded, "Pauline" and "Paracelsus," and in 1838 Miss Barrett produced, in defiance of the taste of the age, her irregular and impassioned "Seraphim." None of these publications, however, disturbed in the least degree the supremacy of the school of good sense, or threatened that "equipoise of reason" which the disciples of Southey thought that they had fixed for ever. Poetry was to preserve its logical judgment; it was never to "let itself go." The cardinal importance of Bailey's "Festus" is that it was the earliest direct counterblast to this scheme of imaginative discipline, and that when it appeared in 1839 the walls built up by Henry Taylor's arrogant preface immediately began to crumble down.

II

The extraordinary poem which thus recalled English literature to the ecstatic after a period of bondage to the static, and attracted the astonishment of the public by leading a successful revolt against baldness, against what a critic of the time called "the pride of natural barrenness," was the work of an extremely young man. Philip James Bailey was born in Nottingham on April 22, 1816. He was the son of a journalist of an excellent provincial type, a sturdy local politician, antiquary, and philanthropist, himself an amateur in verse, "an inveterate rhymer," we are told, and full of enthusiasm for new ideas as they revealed themselves to active-thinking persons in those repressed and stunted thirties. The father of Philip James Bailey promptly acquiesced, like the father of Robert Browning, in the decision of his son to adopt "the vocation of a poet," and the boy seems to have been educated to that end, as others to become chartered accountants or solicitors. Nominally, indeed, the latter profession was selected for young Bailey, who, nevertheless, as early as 1835, is understood to have begun to plan his great poem. It is further related that in 1836—the young man was in his twentieth year—he began to write "Festus," and in 1838 had finished the first draft of it.

So far as it appears, there was nothing but irresistible vocation and a selective use of the most sympathetic models which led Bailey back to what had so long and so completely been neglected in English poetry, the record of the subtler action of the mind. In the midst of a fashion for scrupulous common sense and "the equipoise of reason," here was a young man of twenty who, without any sort of impetus from without, and in defiance of current criticism, devoted himself to the employment of clothing philosophic speculation with almost reckless imagery. Henry Taylor had entreated the poets not to attempt to describe anything which cannot "be seen through the mere medium of our eyesight." But from the very outset the new bard was to deal wholly with impassioned spiritual life, exalted into a sphere unoccupied except by rapture and vision. You are to build, practically dictated the Preface of "Philip van Artevelde," nothing but comfortable two-storied villas, with all the modern appliances. The architect of "Festus" comes, raising none but pinnacled archangelic mansions high in the unapparent. This was the note of the amazement with which "Festus" was received in 1839. It bore a message of good tidings to spiritual souls starving in a utilitarian desert. It lifted a palm-tree, it unsealed a well in the arid flats of common sense. We cannot, in the light of all that has been written since, appreciate in the least degree what "Festus" was to its earliest readers, unless we bear this in mind. All the yearnings for the unlimited, all the suppressed visions of infinity, all who groped in darkness after the excessive, and the impassioned, and the inconceivable, gathered in tumult and joy to welcome this new voice. James Montgomery wrote that, after reading "Festus," he felt as though he had been eating of the Tree of the Knowledge of Good and Evil.

To realise what it was which hungry visionaries found in the new poem, it is necessary to turn back to what it was which was presented to them in 1839. The first edition of "Festus" is a work of remarkable interest. It is now very rare, and it may safely be said that there is no volume which justifies more completely the passion or mania of the book-collector. For sixty-three years "Festus" has not lacked readers, and edition after edition has steadily supplied a demand. But the "Festus" of 1901 is a very different affair from the volume of the same name of 1839. In the first place, it is very unlike it in size, since it contains about 40,000 verses, while the original edition has something less than 10,000. We shall presently have to describe the extraordinary manner in which Mr. Bailey, during sixty years, steadily added to the bulk of his poem. But the point to dwell on here is that the effect made upon his own generation was not made by the huge and very unwieldy book which one now buys as "Festus" in the shops, but by a poem which was already lengthy, yet perfectly within the bounds of easy reading. It seems essential, if we are to gauge that effect, to turn back to the first edition. This was a large octavo, with no name on the title-page, but with a symbolic back presenting a malignant snake flung downwards through the inane by the rays that dart from a triangle of light, a very proper preparation for the redundant and arcane invocations of the text within the covers.

The attack of the utilitarians had been chiefly directed against the disciples of Byron, and the new poet evaded the censure of such critics by ignoring in the main the influence of that dæmonic enchanter. It is specious to see the effect of "Manfred" upon "Festus," but in point of fact the resemblance seems to result from a common study of "Faust." Nor has the "Dr. Faustus" of Marlowe—although, since the publication of Lamb's "Specimens" in 1808, that majestic poem had been within every one's reach—anything very definite to do with Bailey's conception. This was founded, almost too closely, on that of Goethe's "Faust." The result of the manipulation of later editions has been more and more to disguise the resemblance of the original draft of "Festus" to its great German forerunner, and to this, therefore, with the edition of 1839 before us, we must give a moment's attention.

Bailey's poem began, not as it does now, but with an abrupt introduction of the reader to Heaven, exactly as in "Faust," with a "Prolog im Himmel." In each case God himself speaks, and in a triplet of verses. There is a "Chor der Engel," called by Bailey "Seraphim" and "Cherubim," and these combine in a great burst of melodious adoration, like "die himmelischen Heerschaaren" in "Faust." Lucifer demands the soul of Festus to sport with, exactly as Mephistopheles asks for Faust. When the tempter abruptly appears to his meditating mortal victim, the startled "Who art thou, pray?" of Festus is precisely the "Wie nennst du dich?" of Faust. Later on, Lucifer and Festus ride Ruin and Darkness, the black colts of the Evil One, exactly as Faust and Mephistopheles do their black steeds after the Walpurgisnacht. In the 1839 edition of "Festus" the lyrical element is very much more prominent than in the later editions, where it has been steadily superseded by blank verse. These odes and choruses in the original text are plainly modelled upon the lyrics in the German poem, and, what is curious, it seems to be rather the second than the first part of "Faust" which has attracted the English rhapsodist, whose cantatas occasionally recall, in their form, those of the "Chor seliger Knaben" and the rest.

It would be interesting to trace the mode in which Goethe influenced the mind of the young Nottingham poet, whose masterpiece was to be the most important contribution to English literature in which rivalry with "Faust" is predominant. Bailey, as I am informed, never resided in Germany, and had but a scanty knowledge of the German language. The only direct reference to Goethe which I have found in his writings occurs in "The Age," where he remarks that—

> *Wolfgang's "Faust" flames forth the fire divine*
> *In many a solid thought and glowing line—*

a couplet of not particularly luminous criticism. I suppose that Bailey was not constrained to spell out the original, since, by 1836, Goethe was not without interpreters in this country. The acquaintance of Englishmen with Goethe as a force hardly existed earlier than 1827, when Carlyle's two great essays made their mark. In 1831 Abraham Hayward led the army of translators with a privately printed "Faust," and in 1832 a certain sensation was caused in English intellectual circles by the death of Goethe, a reverberating event. Then followed version upon version, comment upon comment; the publication to the outer world of Hayward in 1833, in 1835 the "Faust" of Dr. Anster, eagerly commended by the *Edinburgh Review*—these, we may shrewdly conjecture, were the main media of inspiration to the youthful Bailey, although he probably glanced at the original. Moreover, there existed a widely circulated portfolio of designs for "Faust" by Ritzsch, with some text in English; these drawings were in the hands of the infant Dante Gabriel Rossetti, it appears, by 1836, and may very well have stimulated the imagination of the adolescent author of "Festus." There can be, at all events, no awkwardness in comprehending that the latter, without any deep knowledge of the German language, but by a mere happy inevitable instinct, could grasp the essential character of the sublime poem of Goethe, and bend its design to his own ends. The difficulty, I confess, to me is that, as I have said, "Festus" seems to presuppose familiarity with some scenes, at least, of the second part of "Faust," which had not been published anywhere until 1831, and was but slowly and confusedly recognised in England.

In the evolution of a plot the English drama was far less successful than its German exemplar. The great disadvantage of "Festus" was immediately perceived to be its lack of coherent outline. Elizabeth Barrett remarked that "the fine things were worth looking for, in the design *manqué*." Horne, one of the earliest and most judicious of admirers, lamented that the framework of the poem was unworthy of its eminent beauties of detail. The plot of "Festus" is, in fact, too slight to bear the heavy robes of brocade which are hung about its insufficiency. To make such a work durably weighty it should have an actual story, complicated and animated enough to arrest attention. This was perfectly comprehended by Goethe in both parts of "Faust." But the narrative element in "Festus" is thin and vague to excess. The hero is a human soul, of the highest gifts and attainments, doomed to despair and melancholy, and unwillingly enslaved to sin. The mode in which he becomes the plaything of the arch-spirit of evil is impressive, but scarcely intelligible; nor are the relations of the tempter to his victim ever realised in a vividly dramatic or narrative way. It would be an almost impossible feat to separate the "story" or plot of "Festus" from its lyrical and rhetorical ornament. One has to face the fact that the poem exists in and for these purple robes, and that it is essentially a series of transcendent visions, each clothed upon by a fresh set of more or less sumptuous and redundant imagery.

The keynote of "Festus" is a spiritual optimism. The lesson of the poem was easily perceived to be insistence upon the ministry of evil as a purifier. Man was to pass through sin as through a fire, and to come out purged from the dross of humanity. At the opening of the poem the note of hope is struck. In spite of Lucifer, and of all his ingenious activity, Earth and Man are improving. But God (the youthful Bailey was extraordinarily familiar with the mind of the Creator), in a speech of disconcerting petulance, dooms Earth to end: "Earth to death is given," and the pitying angels cover their faces. It is by playing upon the depression of one who inhabits an orb which is about to be annihilated that Lucifer obtains his ascendancy over the spirit of Festus; he approaches him in the guise of a giant force, placable and sane, that will give the longed-for happiness. But Festus rejects all the vulgar forms of joy:

> *Spirit,*
> *It is not bliss I seek; I care not for it.*
> *I am above the low delights of life.*
> *The life I live is in a dark cold cavern,*
> *Where I wander up and down, feeling for something*
> *Which is to be; and must be; what, I know not;*
> *But the incarnation of my destiny*
> *Is nigh* . . .
> *The worm of the world hath eaten out my heart.*

Lucifer is equal to the opportunity; he promises to renew the heart of Festus within him, and to endow it with immortality in spite of God. Festus wavers, but he is now launched upon a career of supernatural adventures, presented to us in a succession of scenes and visions. These are pleasing in proportion with their seriousness, for Bailey had none of Goethe's gift of laughter, and his "comic relief" is invariably deplorable. It is in his communion with infinity, in his pictures of impassioned spiritual life, that he is successful, and his flights are most fully to be trusted when they carry him farthest up into the empyrean.

If we analyse the narrative of "Festus," we are led to strange and awkward conclusions. The Spirit of Evil, embodied in Lucifer, rarely coincides with the ethical action of guilt, and is often actually in collision with it. One does not see what Lucifer has to gain from his ascendancy over Festus, since that personage continues melancholy, active in aspiration, in will passionately virtuous. The great evidence of his spiritual peril is the yielding of his intellect to the Devil, but Bailey is too delicate to carry out this submission to any practical issue. If Lucifer is very audacious, Festus does not embrace the wicked suggestion, but turns and rates the tempter, in tones dignified and courteous, like those of Dr. Primrose reproving sin in Mr. Thornhill. On their Walpurgisnacht-ride over the world Festus and Lucifer overhear an island-people, on their knees before a maiden fair, singing " Hail, Victoria! Princess, hail!" (A.D. 1837), and quaintly enough it seems to be gratitude to Lucifer for having shown him this patriotic scene which finally conquers the scruples of Festus and binds him to the tempter.

The central incidents of the poem are sometimes difficult to follow. Lucifer takes Festus up into the planet Venus, where they have an interview with the Muse, and where Angela, the dead love of

Festus, appears to him. The scene changes to earth, and Festus is discovered with one "my Helen" at what the stage-direction calls "a large party and entertainment." This episode, or lyrical intermezzo, is long, and breaks the poem into two parts; it was considered very sprightly in the forties. Festus sings the following song at supper :

> *Thy nature is so pure and fine,*
>   *'Tis most like wine;*
> *Thy blood, which blushes thro' each vein,*
>   *Rosy champagne;*
> *And the fair skin which o'er it grows,*
>   *Bright as its snows.*
> *Thy wit, which thou dost work so well,*
>   *Is like cool moselle;*
> *Like madeira, bright and warm,*
>   *Is thy smile's charm;*
> *Claret's glory hath thine eye,*
>   *Or mine must lie;*
> *But nought can like thy lip possess*
>   *Deliciousness!*
> *And now that thou art divinely merry,*
> *I'll kiss and call thee, sparkling sherry.*

When Bailey is "divinely merry" he puts the Muses out of countenance; yet this amazing anacreontic has survived through all the editions of "Festus." The social occasion which opens with this gaiety proves a very lengthy and animated affair; there are rompings and singing of arch songs, and the discomfortable practice of wearing, beneath the lamp, wreaths of flowers which have been dipped in the wine-cup, much prevails. An extraordinary number of kisses, and vows, and amorous forfeits are exchanged, and Lucifer takes a modest and agreeable part in the entertainment. But at Nottingham, in the reign of William IV., the most successful evening parties came to an end before midnight, and one George having gone so far as to propose that a certain Fanny should "fold him bee-like on her bosom's gentle tide," both Festus and Lucifer feel that it is time to separate, and the latter proposes that George should "shake hands, man, with eternity," or, in other words, should go home to bed. The stage-direction is, "They break up."

From these faded pleasantries it is strange to turn to the serious portions of the poem, which have preserved to a remarkable degree their freshness and sonority. Almost immediately after this "party," so unhappy in its provinciality, we come upon a scene admirably dramatic in tone, and in its excellent ironic note of mockery not unworthy of Goethe or of Ibsen, in which Lucifer, in the guise of a ranter at the door of a church, preaches to the crowd a sermon on predestination, fooling his audience savagely, till, at last, they perceive his intention and turn to kill him. There is nothing of its kind finer in the poetry of that age than this magnificent sermon where it turns from persiflage to contemptuous invective. "Tremble!" cries Lucifer to his conventional congregation—

Tremble! ye dare not believe.
No, cowards! sooner than believe ye would die.
Die with the black lie flapping on your lips
Like the soot-flake upon a burning bar.
Be merry, happy if ye can: think never
Of him who slays your souls, nor Him who saves,—
There's time enough for that when you're a-dying!

Men are not to resist—such is the gospel of Lucifer ; let yourselves go, he preaches, be swept on. Resistance is the beginning of spiritual life, it gives God his chance for leverage. "Prance merrily off, skim like bubbles on the river, for then you are sure to come to me." This is very Goethesque : "stürzt euch in Peneios',Fluth !" one remembers.

Although the subject is so audacious and apocalyptical, the text of the first edition of "Festus" is remarkable for simplicity of diction. There is a general absence of pomposity ; the author is inspired, with evident earnestness, by a genuine ecstasy of spiritual life. He submits to "visions of sublime convocation," but he avoids the error of translating these into swollen and preposterous language. It is the more needful to insist on this because in later editions Bailey contrived to spoil his poem in this respect. He lost a great deal of his directness of speech, and he substituted for it, as we shall presently see, a bombastic splendour which did him grievous wrong. But the blank verse of the original "Festus," which has something of the best parts of Young's "Night Thoughts" (that very stately piece of elaborate rhetoric, nowadays so unjustly decried), is plain, full, and direct, with curious touches of realism. Its lyrics are less happy. Sometimes, as in the ballad of "The Gipsy Maid," we have such a vivid improvisation as we could imagine a bard composing by a watch-fire in a mountain-pass, with no art, no care, yet with a long breath of melancholy music. But, in the main, it is the non-lyrical parts of "Festus" which fascinate its readers now, as they did those of sixty years ago, by their unsatisfied yearnings after infinity, their enfranchised metaphysical speculation, and their uplifted clarion-cries of melody and vision.

III

Reviewers of the prevailing school, who held that poetry should be rational, broad, and calm, received "Festus" in 1839 with bewilderment. To some of them it seemed less an achievement in art than an exercise in theological mysticism run mad. But the general verdict of the best judges was highly favourable, and when it became known that it was the production of a youth of two-and-twenty, it was looked upon as a kind of portent.

There seemed nothing preposterous in comparing such a work with the famous monuments of literary precocity, with the "Ode on Christ's Nativity," with the "Essay on Criticism," with "Endymion." What might not the author attain to? It could not be questioned that "Festus" was a better poem than "Queen Mab"; why should young Bailey not grow up to be as great a poet as Shelley? Already he possessed sustained powers of a very high order. He had actually achieved, at these his tender years, a body of philosophical verse strenuous, fervent, and elevated. He had already, as Swift might have said, his wings and his music. What he lacked was what youth never possesses, a sense of proportion, a delicacy of workmanship, a full command over his materials. These would naturally follow with the ripening years, "which mellow what we write to the dull sweets of rhyme."

By what inscrutable fate was it ordained that in this case the gifts never ripened at all? At twenty-three Bailey was perhaps the most "promising" of living English poets, and at eighty-six that promise was still to be fulfilled. In 1902, as in 1839, Philip James Bailey was the author of "Festus," neither more nor less. Had he died in the last-mentioned year he would have retained a foremost place among our "inheritors of unfulfilled renown"; he would be habitually mentioned with Chatterton. But, by the oddest irony, he survived, actively endeavouring to improve his position, until extreme old age, and yet was never able to recapture his earliest melody and fervour. Meanwhile his arrested development and successive mishaps did not affect to any appreciable degree the fate of his solitary production, which continued and continues still to have a wide circle of readers. The case is odd in itself and singular in the history of our literature.

The earliest reception of "Festus" was mainly by those most intimately interested in the art of poetry. Tennyson, Bulwer Lytton, Thackeray, the Brownings, and Horne were among its few original admirers and advocates. But as time went on, the ring of readers spread further outwards and became steadily less esoteric. The edition of 1846, which bore the author's name on the title-page, greatly added to the quantity of his readers, but took something from their quality. Tennyson, who had been rapturous, while advising FitzGerald to read "Festus"—"There are really *very grand* things in it"—confessed that his correspondent would "most likely find it a great bore." (Any human being, by the way, less likely to appreciate "Festus" than FitzGerald it would be difficult to imagine.) The Brownings, even, now saw spots in the sun. But with this slackening of technical or professional interest in Bailey there grew up a public sympathy founded on the matter of his poem, its theological positions, its doctrine of ultimate salvation, its bewitching theory of remedial chastisement, its universalism. This process of divorce from the purely literary current of the time has continued ever since, and is the cause of several of the anomalies of Bailey's celebrity.

Borne on a tide of imaginative earnestness, the young author had declared that whatever he had received, in a rush of improvisation, was made independent of the workmanlike attributes of the art by the fullness of his message and the abundance of his imagery. With incomparable boldness this lad of twenty-three had written as the colophon of his poem :

> *Read this, world! He who writes is dead to thee,*
> *But still lives in these leaves. He spake inspired:*
> *Night and day, thought came unhelped, undesired,*
> *Like blood to his heart.*

This is an impressive attitude, so long as the inspiration lasts ; but suppose it to be withdrawn ? It is then that the rhapsodist feels the lack of that craft and discipline of art which he scorned in the hour of his prophetic afflatus. There was never a greater disappointment than attended the publication of Bailey's second volume, " The Angel World," in 1850. The opportunity was matchless, since a generation had now grown up emancipated from all the sedative legislation of Southey and Taylor. Highly coloured poetry was at present in fashion ; imagination had reasserted its supremacy over reason. There was no fear that Bailey's verse would be reproved because of its excess of force and fervour. But "The Angel World," to use Jeffrey's phrase, "wouldn't do." It was a kind of celestial romance in blank verse, faintly reminiscent of "Eloa" and still more faintly of "The Loves of the Angels." It repeated, in less seductive accents, the universalist dogma of "Festus"—good and bad alike were finally to be lapped in the mantle of the Eternal rest :

> *They who had erred and they who taught to err,*
> *Along with those who, wise and pure, withstood.*

But it was, either as a tale or as a sermon, extraordinarily unexhilarating. However, although the little volume has never been re-issued, the reader may in this matter indolently form his own opinion, since Bailey, finding that people would not accept "The Angel World," formed an ingenious and unfortunate project, which he continued to carry out for the rest of his life. If a poem was received by the critics and the public with marked disfavour, he would be even with them by putting it bodily into the next edition of "Festus." The argument in his mind seems to have been something like this: " You won't read my new piece, and you say you prefer 'Festus'? Very well, then it shall form part of 'Festus,' and so you will be obliged to read it." Accordingly, as research will prove, "The Angel World" was broken into two parts, and was silently implanted in the middle of the next edition of "Festus," with such verbal adaptations as were necessary, but otherwise without change.

Internal evidence tends to show that the crushing failure of "The Angel World" convinced the poet of his error in depending wholly on improvisation or "inspiration." In 1855 he published "The Mystic," a volume which displays a close preoccupation with form. It consists of three unrelated poems, of which the first is modelled on Shelley's "Alastor," while the second, called "A Spiritual Legend," is a strenuous and almost violent *pastiche* of Miltonic blank verse, the stresses and inversions and elisions of the rhythm of "Paradise Lost" being reproduced as though for a wager. In particular, the Miltonic use of proper names is introduced without restraint, so as to produce at length an almost ludicrous effect, although often in itself beautiful in its full echo of Milton:

> *By great Shedaa, city occult, whose walls*
> *Towered in alternate tiers of silver and gold;*
> *Where bright Herat, city of roses, lights*
> *With dome and minaret the landskip green;*
> *Damasek old, old Byblos, or Babel,*
> *Or Tchelminar, or Baalbek, or where Balkh,*
> *Mother of cities, murally encrowned,*
> *Mourns.*

There are magnificent lines in both these poems, but especially in "A Spiritual Legend." The fault of them is their obscurity, their vagueness; it is, frankly, impossible to know what "The Mystic" is all about. It must be considered mainly as an exercise in versification, undertaken, oddly and perhaps pathetically, by a poet who felt that something divine, a gift of youth, was slipping from him, and who determined to recapture it by a tardy and vain preoccupation with the form and structure of verse.

Certain fragments of the volume of 1855 were shredded, in the extraordinary fashion already mentioned, into the ever-swelling "Festus," although most of "The Mystic" was rebellious to this kind of adaptation. But Bailey had formed the idea, long before this, that the original outline of "Festus" was sufficiently elastic to be stretched indefinitely:

"more or less"—ambiguous phrase!—he had perceived this from the beginning, he wrote in 1889. He worked everything into the design of his drama; he accounted for all his later fancies and rhapsodies by thinking "This will do for 'Festus.'" He thought that there had been revealed to him a new and more rational idea of Hell, and he now scarcely wrote anything in which his ideas of the limitation of punishment and the eternity of universal bliss did not find place. A curious example of this persistency may be given. The last of the three pieces which form the volume of 1855 is a ballad called "A Fairy Tale"; it is one of Bailey's least fortunate productions, a languid and insipid story of how a little girl was disporting at eve in a verdant ring, when she was pounced down upon by the fairies, and persuaded to live with them. The hasty reader might easily see in this nothing but a piece of unusually guileless and puerile early Victorian mock-romance, but if he pushes on he will find his Bailey. The little girl casually discovers that the fairies are greatly dejected by their lack of a soul, so she sits up at the flower-embroidered banquet and eloquently propounds to Sir Oberon and to "divine Titania, night's incomparable queen," the glad theory of universal salvation. It really became with Bailey a King Charles's head.

Of the later publications of Bailey it is kinder not to speak in detail. "The Age," of 1858, was a satire on the manners and morals of the day, in heroic couplets; "Universal Hymn," in Thomsonian blank verse, of 1867, was cut up in the usual way, to feed that poetical Oliver Twist, the insatiable "Festus"; "Nottingham Castle," of 1878, was an attempt at an historical ode in the grand style. No poet ever did more in his later years to destroy the favourable impression created by the writings of his youth. For the last quarter of a century Mr. Bailey gave up the vain attempt to attract readers to his miscellaneous writings. He frankly abandoned them, and we deed not dwell upon them. He could afford to throw these punier children of his brain to the wolves, because of the really formidable proportions which his first-born had gradually attained. To a recent visitor he said, plainly, that he was the author of one book, and that is what he will remain in the chronicle of literature. His obstinate determination to present his string of scenes as a whole, in spite of the hopelessly invertebrate character of the design, has in the end led to a sort of acceptation of "Festus" as a definite achievement.

IV

Of attempts to "place" the author of "Festus" in relation to other authors, the earliest, so far as I am able to discover, was that made by Robert Chambers in 1858. This careful critic, surveying the literature of his day, observed "a group of philosophical poets—men of undoubted talent, learning, and poetic imagination, but too often obscure, mystical, and extravagant." This group, he explained, consisted of P. J. Bailey, Robert Browning, and Richard Hengist Horne. To-day the differences between "Festus," "Paracelsus," and "Orion" are more striking than the similarities, but Bailey had a pronounced admiration for both the latter poems. For the Brownings Mr. Bailey preserved an enthusiastic regard, but there is no trace of their style upon his.[1] In fact, we look in vain for contemporary influences in "Festus"; Goethe for matter, Milton, Thomson, and Shelley for manner, were Bailey's masters, and occasionally he was faintly touched by Byron. It will be found that what was ultimately discarded from "Festus" as immature is in the main Byronic. The prevailing Byronism was a weed which he uprooted from his poetic garden, as Tennyson and Browning are said to have done from theirs.

Mr. Bailey's interest in the successive generations which he saw rise up and pass away was kindly but fluctuating. He liked a gorgeous texture in poetry, and was therefore attracted to D. G. Rossetti and much later to Lord de Tabley. About 1870-75 he indulged, anonymously, in a certain amount of reviewing, and said very kind and delicate things about some of the poets that were at that time

[1] Miss F. C. Carey, the niece and constant companion of Mr. Bailey, tells me that her uncle became acquainted with "Paracelsus" soon after the publication of "Festus," probably in 1840, as the gift of Westland Marston. This disposes of any idea of the influence of the earlier on the later poem.

making their first bow to the public. But more interesting is the fact that in the fifties he was taken as a model by a group of writers who made a great stir for a moment, and are now too readily forgotten. These were the Spasmodists, as they were called, who accepted the rather formless "Festus" as the pattern for huge semi-dramatic pieces more amorphous still; Alexander Smith, in "A Life Drama" (1853), Sydney Dobell, in "Balder" (1854), and John Stanyan Bigg, in "Night and the Soul" (1854), displayed themselves as the docile and reverent offspring of Bailey. Why the influence of "Festus" suddenly, after so many years, made its appearance thus sown broadcast is curious, and curious too the extravagance of these imitations. Perhaps no one ever soared and sank so violently as did the author of "Night and the Soul." Yet even the Spasmodists had merits, which might detain a critic, but here they are interesting to us only as a cluster of satellites oddly circling round the planet of "Festus" in its mid-career.

The Spasmodists imitated Mr. Bailey's ecstasy, but not his moral earnestness and not his original strain of religious philosophy. His was a mind of greater weight and fuller body than theirs. He was often redundant and sometimes nebulous, but there was always something definite behind the coloured cloud. His occasional excursions into prose were not fortunate, for his style was awkward and heavy, and he liked to coin impossible words: he says "evilhood," for instance, although even he seems to have blenched before the use of "goodhood." His prose was unattractive, therefore, but it is worth examining, because it reveals the intense convictions which led the writer onward. In natural temperament, I think, Mr. Bailey was timid, but in his determination to thrust his message on the world he showed an absolute courage which neither ridicule, nor argument, nor neglect could shake in the slightest degree. And this may bring us to a reflection to which the study of "Festus" must inevitably lead, namely, that in this his single-minded earnestness lay the secret of Mr. Bailey's reward. A word to indicate in what way this operated must close this brief study of his work and character.

With a curious misuse of a phrase which has become almost a journalistic *cliché*, Bailey has been recently called a "poet's poet." If this term has a meaning at all, it refers to the quality which makes certain writers, whose nature leads them to peculiar delicacy of workmanship, favourites with their fellow-craftsmen, although little comprehended by the vulgar. Mr. Bailey was the exact opposite of these poets. There was nothing in his work to attract students of what is exquisitely put, and, as a rule, he has been little appreciated by these rarer spirits. His form is so plain as to be negligible; it is in his matter, in his ethical attitude, that he is found attractive by those—and they are numerous—who in several generations have come under his spell. "Festus" appeals to the non-literary temperament, which is something very different indeed from saying that it appeals to the anti-literary. Those who love it appreciate its imagery, its large music, its spacious landscape, but they value it mainly for its teaching. No purely æsthetic estimate of the poem will satisfy those who reply, " Yes, what you say is technically true, no doubt ; but it has helped and comforted me, and it helps me still." In many a distant home, in America even oftener than in Great Britain, a visit to some invalid's room would reveal the presence of two volumes on the bed the one a Bible, the other " Festus." This is an element in the popularity of Philip James Bailey which criticism is powerless to analyse. But no consideration of his remarkable career is complete if a record of it is neglected.

1902

"ORION" HORNE
1802–1884

"ORION" HORNE

THE publication of the love letters which passed, in 1845 and 1846, between Robert Browning and Elizabeth Barrett blew a little of the dust off several names which were brightly before the public then and have become sadly obscured since. The two learned lovers speak of Mr. Serjeant Talfourd and of his incomparable tragedy of "Ion," of Sir John Hanmer and his sonnets, of the terrible criticisms of Chorley, of the writings of Abraham Heraud and Silk Buckingham and Cornelius Mathews. These are faded notorieties with a vengeance. But amongst these names, faintly echoing from the earliest Victorian period, we meet with one more than the rest deserving of perpetuation, with at all events a greater mass of actually accomplished work attached to it, the name of Mr. Horne, the author of "Cosmo de Medici," of "Gregory VII.," and, above all, of "the farthing epic," the once extremely celebrated "Orion." And with this there comes vividly back to me a vision of an extraordinary personage, of whom I saw a great deal in my youth, and of whom I feel disposed to garner some of my impressions before I lose them.

He had been baptized Richard Henry Horne, but in late middle life he had changed the second of these names to Hengist. It was in 1874 that I set eyes on him first, in circumstances which were somewhat remarkable. The occasion was the marriage of the poet, Arthur O'Shaughnessy, to the eldest daughter of Westland Marston, the playwright. There was a large and distinguished company present, and most of the prominent "Pre-Raphaelites," as they were still occasionally called. In the midst of the subsequent festivities, and when the bride was surrounded by her friends, a tiny old gentleman cleared a space around him, and, all uninvited, began to sit upon the floor and sing, in a funny little cracked voice, Spanish songs to his own accompaniment on the guitar. He was very unusual in appearance. Although he was quite bald at the top of his head, his milk-white hair was luxuriant at the sides, and hung in clusters of ringlets. His moustache was so long that it became whisker, and in that condition drooped, also in creamy ringlets, below his chin. The elder guests were inclined to be impatient, the younger to ridicule this rather tactless interruption. Just as it seemed possible something awkward would happen, Robert Browning stepped up and said, in his loud, cheerful voice: "That was charming, Horne! It quite took us to 'the warm South'' again," and cleverly leading the old gentleman's thoughts to a different topic, he put an end to the incident.

This scene was very characteristic of Horne, who was gay, tactless, and vain to a remarkable degree. He had lately come back from Australia, where nothing had gone well with him for long together, and he did not understand the ways of the younger generation in London. But to those who could be patient with his peculiarities he offered a very amusing study. He had delightful stories, many of which are still inedited, of the great men of his youth—Wordsworth, Hunt, Hazlitt, in particular. But he himself, with his incredible mixture of affectation and fierceness, humour and absurdity, enthusiasm and ignorance, with his incoherency of appearance, at once so effeminate and so muscular, was better than all his tales. He was a combination of the troubadour and the prize-fighter, on a miniature scale. It was impossible not to think of a curly white poodle when one looked at him, especially when he would throw his fat little person on a sofa and roll about, with gestures less dignified than were, perhaps, ever before seen in a poet of between seventy and eighty years of age. And yet he had a fine, buoyant spirit, and a generous imagination with it all. But the oddity of it, alas! is what lingers in the memory—those milky ringlets, that extraordinary turn of the head, that embrace of the beribboned guitar!

In a pathetic little letter which Horne wrote to me in his eightieth year, he said, quite placidly, that though he was now forgotten, no poet had ever had more pleasant things said of him by people dead and gone. It was perfectly true. Wordsworth and Tennyson, Leigh Hunt and Walter Savage Landor, had all praised his poetry; Carlyle had declared that "the fire of the stars was in him," and G. H. Lewes that he was "a man of the most unquestionable genius." How highly Robert and Elizabeth Browning regarded him may be seen over and over again in the course of their correspondence. But his talent was of a very fugitive kind. He was a remarkable poet for seven or eight years, and a tiresome and uninspired scribbler for the rest of his life. His period of good work began in 1837, when he published "Cosmo de Medici" and "The Death of Marlowe"; it closed in 1843, with the publication of "Orion," and the composition of all that was best in the "Ballad Romances." If any one wished to do honour to the *manes* of poor old Horne—and in these days far less distinguished poets than he receive the hònours of rediscovery—the way to do it would be to publish in one volume the very best of his writings, and nothing more. The badness of the bulk of his later verse is outside all calculation. How a man who had once written so well as he, could ever come to write, for instance, "Bible Tragedies" (1881) is beyond all skill of the literary historian to comprehend.

But, although Horne was, for a short time, a good poet, he was always more interesting as a human being. His whole life was an adventure; it was like a "book for boys." He was pleased to relate that even his birth was not ordinary, for he came into the world so exactly at the stroke of midnight on the last day of the year that it could never be decided whether he was born in 1802 or 1803. I do not know who his parents were or what his family. In the days when I saw so much of him he appeared to be quite solitary; he never spoke of possessing a relative. He was trained for the army, and lost his chance through some foolish escapade. But before this he had been at school at Enfield, where Tom Keats, the poet's brother, and Charles Wells, who wrote "Joseph and his Brethren," had been his school-fellows. He used to tell us in his old age that he was once scampering out of school, when he saw the chaise of Mr. Hammond, the surgeon, standing at the door. John Keats, who was Hammond's apprentice, was holding the horse, his head sunken forward in a brown study; the boys, who knew how pugnacious Keats was, dared Horne to throw a snowball at him, which Horne did, hitting Keats in the back of the head, and then escaping round the corner at a headlong pace. It used to be very thrilling, in the eighties, to hear the old gentleman tell how he had actually snowballed Keats; almost as though one should arise and say that he had sold Shakespeare a cheese-cake.

Just before he should have entered Sandhurst the young Horne was lured away to America, and offered himself as a volunteer in the War of Mexican Independence. He entered the new Mexican navy as a midshipman, and dashed about under irregular fire at the bombardment of Vera Cruz and at the siege of San Juan Ulloa. He used to tell us that he never would miss his swim in the sea in the morning, nor return to the ship until he had been well within range of the guns of Vera Cruz. The Spaniards could never hit him, he said; but one day when he was making a long nose at the gunners, he was as nearly as possible swallowed from behind by a shark. I forget how he accounted for his escape, but there was always a good deal of Baron Munchausen about Mr. Horne.

When the Mexican War was over, he strolled across the United States, with a belt full of doubloons girded about his person, and visited the Mohawks, the Oneidas, and the Hurons. He had a fight with a Red Indian brave and beat him, and carried away a bunch of eagle-feathers from his body. After many strange adventures, he must needs bathe in public under the cataract of Niagara. Two of his ribs were found to be broken when he was fished out again, insensible. He then took a steerage passage in a steamer that was wrecked in the St. Lawrence. He walked in moccasins over to Halifax, Nova Scotia, and started again in a timber ship, whose crew rose in mutiny and set fire to her in mid-Atlantic; Mr. Horne quelled the mutiny and put out the fire, to the eternal gratitude of the captain, who fell upon his knees upon the deck and kissed his hands. I delighted in Mr. Horne's stories of his past life, but sometimes I used to fear that he exaggerated.

It was not until he was thirty years of age that Horne began to take up literature, and he was thirty-five when he enjoyed his first success with "Cosmo de Medici," an historical tragedy in blank verse, which has some very fine passages, and was greatly admired in the London coteries. Then came the period of seven years, of which I have spoken, in which Horne really took his place, with Browning and Tennyson, as one of the promising poets of the age. If he had died in 1844, he would probably hold a high place still, as an "inheritor of unfulfilled renown," but unfortunately he lived for forty more years, and never discovered that his talent had abandoned him. His "Orion," which was published in 1843, was brought out at the price of one farthing. Elizabeth Barrett sent out to the nearest bookshop for a shilling's worth, but was refused her four dozen copies. Purchasers had to produce their brass farthing for each "Orion," and no change was given. This was done "to mark the public contempt into which epic poetry has fallen," but it was also a very good advertisement. Everybody talked about Mr. Horne's "farthing" poem, and after some editions had run out the price was cautiously raised. But when the tenth edition appeared, at a cost of seven shillings, the public perceived that its leg was being pulled, and it purchased "Orion" no more. In spite of all this, "Orion" is far indeed from being a humorous composition; it is a dignified and melodious romance of Greek symbolism, with some remote relation to the "Hyperion" of Keats, and contains some admirable passages.

The poets of the opening years of Queen Victoria's reign were almost all of them tempted to write philosophical poetry. Robert Browning had led the way with "Pauline" and "Paracelsus." Bailey had produced "Festus"; Ragg, the lace-worker (now forgotten), had made a temporary mark with "The Deity," a formidable essay; Miss Barrett wrote "The Drama of Exile"; there were the lucubrations of John Edmund Reade. None of these laborious poems could be styled successful, but they all were interesting in their curious contemporary effort to reconcile ideas with sensations, on a grand scale. These writers believed that unless a poem contained a philosophy it was, on the whole, a poor affair. Horne joined the band of the philosophers when he wrote "Orion," which is perhaps, as a poem, the best of the group. His mind was not disciplined, but he always had a curiosity about the literature of thought. He made the acquaintance, about 1841, of a doctor of philosophy, Dr. Leonard Schmitz, who came over from Bonn to introduce German literature to English readers. Conversation with Schmitz set Horne's thoughts running in the direction of a poem which should re-establish the union which had existed in ancient times between philosophy and poetry, before analysis stepped in and divorced them. The effort was one quite beyond Horne's power to carry out successfully, but he wrote what is by no means the worst of modern machines.

This is the poet's explanation of his "spiritual epic," as Elizabeth Barrett called it, as it appeared to him thirty years afterwards :

"Orion, the hero of my fable, is meant to present a type of the struggle of man with himself—that is to say, the contest between the intellect and the senses, when powerful energies are equally balanced. Orion is man standing naked before Heaven and Destiny, resolved to work as a really free agent to the utmost pitch of his powers for the good of his race. He is a truly practical believer in his gods and in his own conscience; a man with the strength of a giant; innocently wise; with a heart expanding towards the largeness and warmth of Nature, and a spirit unconsciously aspiring to the stars. He is a dreamer of noble dreams and a hunter of grand shadows (in accordance with the ancient symbolic myth), all tending to healthy thought or to practical action and structure. He is the type of a Worker and a Builder for his fellow-men."

There is in this commentary a touch of the teaching of Carlyle, who in his turn perused "Orion" with marked affability. The sage of Chelsea had recently published "Heroes and Hero-worship," which had no warmer admirer than Horne. "Orion," then, the "farthing epic," appeared with every circumstance in its favour and enjoyed a very considerable success. Why it is no longer read it would be difficult to say. Its lustrous descriptions of primeval giants are solemn and beautiful, but unfortunately the memory goes back to "Hyperion." Yet this is unjust, and it would be puzzling to define what it is that makes so very careful and accomplished a work not any longer easy to read, in spite of its excellent proportions, moderate length, and indisputable dignity. The "deliberate opinion" of Edgar Allan Poe was that "in all that regards the loftiest and holiest attributes of true poetry 'Orion' has never been excelled." It is certainly very good; listen :

> *Ye rocky heights of Chios, where the snow,*
> *Lit by the far-off and receding moon,*
> *Now feels the soft dawn's purpling twilight creep*
> *Over your ridges, while the mystic dews*
> *Swarm down and wait to be instinct with gold*
> *And solar fire!—ye mountains waving brown*
> *With thick-winged woods, and blotted with deep caves*
> *In secret places; and ye paths that stray*
> *E'en as ye list; what odours and what sighs*
> *Tend your sweet silence through the star-showered night,*
> *Like memories breathing of the Goddess-forms*
> *That left your haunts, yet with the day return.*

Excellent, until we come to the last two lines, which are invaded by that curious flatness characteristic of English poetry in the unfortunate reign of King William IV. When Douglas Jerrold said that Horne had "presented an undying gift to the world" in "Orion," he forgot to estimate the element of decomposition involved in the language of all metrical writers between Keats and Tennyson. Darley, Wade, Wells, Bailey, Heraud, and Beddoes —they all had the unfortunate crack in the voice which made them, with their wealth of enthusiasm for the grand style, incapable of carrying it out without incessant lapses into mediocrity of expression. And Horne, to use a vulgar expression, is tarred with the same William IV. brush. Yet there are very good things in "Orion," lines such as :

> *'Tis always morning somewhere in the world,*

and passages of Greek landscape, of which this is by no means an isolated example :

> *since the breath of spring had stirred the woods,*
> *Through which the joyous tidings busily ran,*
> *And oval buds of delicate pink and green*
> *Broke, infant-like, through bark of sapling boughs,—*
> *The vapours from the ocean had ascended,*
> *Fume after fume, wreath after wreath, and floor*
> *On floor, till a grey curtain upward spread*
> *From sea to sky, and both as one appeared.*
> *Now came the snorting and intolerant steeds*
> *Of the Sun's chariot towards the summer signs ;*
> *At first obscurely, then with dazzling beams,*

and so on. And, as some one has said of Lamartine's efforts in the same kind, there is throughout "Orion," if not a philosophy, at all events a creditable movement of philosophical reflection.

It is known to Apollo only what varied employments Horne took up when the Muses began to abandon him. He was sub-editor of *Household Words* under Dickens, and special commissioner of the *Daily News* to Ireland when the great famine broke out. Suddenly, and desperately determined to marry, he went down to stay with Miss Mitford in Berkshire, and proposed to all the neighbouring heiresses one after another, to the intense indignation of that lady, who declared that he had used her hospitable dining-room, on the same day, to propose to a lady (with £50,000 a year) at lunch, and to another (with £40,000 a year) at tea. None of these efforts was crowned with success; perhaps he had the presumption to be in love with Elizabeth Barrett, whom he had at that time never seen, although oceans of correspondence had passed between them. At all events, directly Robert Browning had carried off his eminent bride, Horne appeared with a little Miss Foggs upon his arm, whom he presently married. They did not get on together; why should history conceal the fact, when Horne himself was wont to dilate upon it so freely to his friends? Mrs. Horne, in tears, threw herself upon the paternal sympathy of Charles Dickens, and Horne indignantly sought a southern hemisphere.

In Australia he was commander of the Gold Escort, and it was delightful, years afterwards, to hear him tell how he convoyed several tons of bullion from Ballarat to Melbourne amid every circumstance of peril. Then he became Gold Commissioner to the Government, but here his flow of high spirits carried him away. He then flung himself into the cultivation of the cochineal insect, edited a Victorian newspaper, became Commissioner of Waterworks, gave lessons in gymnastics, professed the art of natation, and was one of the starters of Australian wine-growing. Long afterwards, when the first Australian cricketers came over to England, Horne wrote to me : " I learn that the cricketers have made each £1000 over here ! Why, oh ! why did not I become an Australian cricketer, instead of an unprofitable swimmer ? When years no longer smiled upon my balls and runs, I might have retired upon my laurelled bat, and have published tragedies at my own expense. Is there any redress for these things in another world ? I don't think so ; I shall be told I had my choice." He certainly paid his money. No one, I suppose, ever failed in so many brilliant, unusual enterprises, every one of which was sure to succeed when he adopted it.

When he came back from Australia, I think about 1869, he was in very low water. He had managed very deeply to offend Charles Dickens, who had taken up the cause of Horne's neglected wife. What happened to Horne in the early years after his return I never heard ; I fancy that he went abroad again for some part of the time. A little later Robert Browning, who had always felt a sincere regard for Horne, was able to be of practical service to him. He was encouraged to republish his poems, and to appeal by means of them to the new age. In these days one used to meet him at afternoon parties, carrying with great care, under his arm, the precious guitar, which he called "my daughter," and was used ceremoniously to introduce as "Miss Horne." A little later in the evening Horne would be discovered on a low stool, warbling Mexican romances, or murmuring with exaggerated gallantry to the prettiest girl in the room. All this time he was thirsting for publicity—if he could only be engaged to sing in public, to box in public, to swim in public, how happy he would be! It used to be said that when he was nearly seventy Horne persuaded the captain of a ship to tie his legs together and fling him into the sea, and that he swam with ease to the boat. A wonderful little ringleted athlete, no doubt!

A great deal of Horne's work in verse, and even in prose, remains unpublished, and is not very likely, I should think, to be ever printed. As I have said, his faculty, which had been so graceful, faded away from him about forty years before he died. When he was in Australia he wrote a good deal, among other things a choral drama, "Prometheus, the Fire-Bringer," which was actually composed out in the bush, and lost, and written all over again, still in the bush. The first edition of this poem is styled "by Richard *Henry* Horne," and the second, which followed soon after, "by Richard *Hengist* Horne," showing the period at which he adopted the more barbaric name. I have glanced through a mass of Horne's manuscript, which I possess (I believe that Mr. Buxton Forman possesses a great deal more), to see whether I can find anything unpublished which is good enough to offer to the readers of this volume. The following impromptu is at least brief; it was composed when the poet was in his seventy-eighth year:

THE SPRING-TIDE OF THE BARDS

Ah, where is the Spring-tide of Poets of old,
 When Chaucer lov'd April and all her sweet showers,
When Spenser's knights felt not their armour strike cold,
 Tho' lost in wet forests or dreaming in bowers?
'Tis a far other planet to us in this season,
And Nature must own we complain with some reason!

For north winds, and east winds, and yellow-fac'd fogs,
 And thunders and lightnings that scare buds and shoots,
May cheer the hoarse chorus of cold-blooded frogs,
 But Man craves life's future, and fears for its fruits.
Then come again, Spring, like the dear songs of old,
Where the crocus smiled daily in sunlight and gold.

Horne's cheerfulness was a very pleasant feature in his character. Life had treated him scurvily, love had missed him, fame had come down and crowned him, and then had rudely snatched the laurel away. If ever a man might have been excused for sourness, it was Horne. But he was a gallant little old man, and if it was impossible not to smile at him, it was still less possible not to recognise his courage and his spirit. Curiously enough, Elizabeth Barrett, who carried on so close a correspondence with Horne in her unmarried days, but who, warned by Miss Mitford, never would allow him to call upon her in person, had an accurate instinct of his merits and his weaknesses, and all the casual remarks about Horne which she makes in the course of her letters to Robert Browning strike one who knew Horne well in later years as singularly exact and perspicacious. His edition of her letters to him, published about twenty years ago in two volumes, is becoming a rare book, and contains many things of remarkable interest and importance.

It was from 1876 to 1879 that we saw him most frequently. He was living at this time in two rooms in Northumberland Street, Regent's Park, in very great poverty, which he bore with the gayest and most gallant *insouciance*. An attempt was made—indeed, several attempts were made—to secure for him a little pension from the Civil List, and these were supported by Carlyle and Browning, Tennyson and Swinburne, to name no smaller fry. But all in vain; for some reason, absolutely inscrutable to me, these efforts were of no avail. It was darkly said that there were reasons why Mr. Gladstone would never, never yield; and he never did. When Lord Beaconsfield came into office, he granted the poor little old man £50 a year, but even then he had not too much food to eat nor clothes to keep him warm. Still he went bravely on, shaking his white ringlets and consoling himself with his guitar. He was fond of mystery, which is a great consoler. For economy's sake, he used to write on post-cards, but always with a great deal of care, so that the postman should be none the wiser. I have such a post-card before me now; it is an answer to a proposal of mine that he should come in and take dinner with us :

"*Nov.* 29, 1877.

"The Sharpshooter's friendly shot just received. By adroitly porting my helm, and hauling out my flying jib, I shall, by 7 o'clock this evening, be able to get the weather-gauge of the Cape I was bound for, and run into your Terrace. Thine.

"REEFER."

Nothing, surely, could be more discreet than that.

To the very last he was anxious to regain his old place as a man of letters, and his persistency was really quite pathetic. One did not know what to do with his suggestions. I appeal to any one acquainted with the business of literature whether anything can be more trying than to receive this sort of communication :

"Don't you think curiosity might be aroused if you could induce the editor of the ——— to print something of this kind : 'We understand that a leading periodical will shortly contain a Dramatic Scene by the Author of "Orion," entitled "The Circle of the Regicides," in which such interlocutors as Dr. Kobold, Prof. Franz Tollkopf, Hans Arbeitsdulder, and Baron Dumm von Ehrsucht will represent certain well-known characters. There will also be brought upon the scene the Apparitions of Brutus, Cromwell, the patriot Mazzini, and the philanthropist Robert Owen; together with a chorus of French and Russian revolutionists, with a trio and chorus of female Regicides.' On second thoughts, perhaps, better stop after 'Owen.'"

It was difficult to bring such suggestions as these within the range of practical literature.

Horne's physical strength was very extraordinary in old age. It was strangely incompatible with the appearance of the little man, with his ringleted locks and mincing ways. But he was past seventy before he ceased to challenge powerful young swimmers to feats of natation, and he very often beat them, carrying off from them cups and medals, to their deep disgust. He was nearly eighty when he filled us, one evening, with alarm by bending our drawing-room poker to an angle in striking it upon the strained muscles of his fore-arm. He was very vain of his physical accomplishments, and he used to declare that he was in training to be a centenarian. These are things that should never be said, they tempt the fates; so one day, just after poor Mr. Horne had been boasting, he was knocked down by a van in Lisson Grove, and, although he rallied in a wonderful way, he was never the same man again. Presently, on March 13, 1884, he died at Margate, whither he had been removed to take the benefit of the sea-air. He was in his eighty-second year. It would be a great pity that a man so unique and so picturesque should be forgotten. As long as the world is interested in Elizabeth Barrett Browning, Horne can never be entirely forgotten, but he deserves to be remembered for his own sake.

AUBREY DE VERE
1814-1902

AUBREY DE VERE

ON January 19, 1902, there passed away in his sleep the most venerable of the then-living poets of the Anglo-Saxon world. There is an old house in County Limerick, with a deer park round it and a lawn that slopes to a lake, all combining to form one of the most exquisite estates in the south of Ireland. There Mr. Aubrey de Vere was born at the beginning of 1814, and there, having reached his eighty-ninth year, he died. It would be impossible to conceive a more gentle, innocent, or delicate life than his was or a more happy one. He did not marry; he consecrated all his activities to the service of literature, and of religion, and of his friends. It was his singular good fortune to be protected from every species of care or anxiety. He was not rich, yet he had the ease and dignity of circumstance which make it possible to concentrate the mind on higher thoughts than surround our daily bread. He was not poor, and yet he was screened by conditions from all that makes the possession of wealth disturbing and hardening. Mr. Aubrey de Vere was more fortunate than the farm-folk in Virgil, for he knew that he was happy. In the moderation of his desires, in the resigning of all vain ambitions, he was as wise as he was pure and good.

Among my treasures I possess a copy of the "Sonnets" of his father, Sir Aubrey de Vere, presented to me by the son, as a kind inscription sets forth, in the year 1869. For the guidance of posterity, however, I have to say that I was not acquainted with Mr. de Vere at so tender an age as this would seem to imply. By one of those slips of the pen which we all make, but which in old age we forget to amend, Mr. de Vere wrote 1869 when he meant 1896. It was, in fact, not until the latter year that I had the privilege of forming an acquaintance which he allowed to ripen into something like a friendship. I met him early in 1896, by special arrangement and in conditions singularly delightful, at the house of an Irish lady who is devoted to literature. The poet was already in his eighty-third year, and my recollections, therefore, are of a very old man. But they are by no means of an infirm or senile man. The mental freshness and buoyancy of his mind continued, I suppose—for I did not see him for several months before his death—almost, if not quite, to the end. They certainly survived, with no symptom of decay, until long after 1896. His letters, which were filled with the enthusiastic love of poetry, continued to breathe the loftiest intellectual ardour even when the implacable years had so shaken the hand that it became difficult to read what was written. This beautiful elasticity of spirit was perhaps the most surprising feature in the wonderful old age of Mr. Aubrey de Vere.

His appearance at about the age of eighty-three is very vivid in my recollection. He entered the room swiftly and gracefully, the front of his body thrown a little forward, as is frequently the case with tall and active old men. His countenance bore a singular resemblance to the portraits of Wordsworth, although the type was softer and less vigorous. His forehead, which sloped a little and was very high and domed, was much observed in the open air from a trick he had of tilting his tall hat back. I used to think, very profanely, that in profile, on these occasions, he bore a quite absurdly close resemblance to the Hatter in " Alice's Adventures," especially when, as was frequently the case, he recited poetry. I am sure that any open-minded person who recollects Mr. de Vere will admit that Sir John Tenniel's immortal drawing of the Hatter repeating "Twinkle, twinkle, little bat!" is irresistibly reminiscent of our revered friend. In spite of this there was something extraordinarily delicate and elevated in his address. He was, in fact, conversation made visible. I never knew a more persistent speaker. If he broke bread with one, the progress of the meal would be interrupted and delayed from the very first by his talk, which was softly, gently unbroken, like a fountain falling upon mosses. On one occasion, when we sat together in a garden in the summer, Mr. de Vere talked, with no other interruption than brief pauses for reflection, for three hours, in itself a prodigious feat for an old man' of eighty-five, and without the smallest sign of fatigue.

In spite of the fact that he occasionally used what are called "strong expressions"—with a little playful affectation, I used to think, of the man of the world —Mr. Aubrey de Vere had an ecclesiastical air, like that of some highly cultivated, imaginative old *abbé*. He possessed a sort of distinguished innocence, a maidenly vivacious brightness, very charming and surprising. He once remarked to me that the feminine characteristics of Newman were always recurring to his memory, that as he looked back upon the early Oxford days he continually had the impression in Newman of "a kind of virginal remoteness mingled with extremely tender grace." When he said this I could not help feeling that although there was no "remoteness" about Mr. de Vere, there was something of the same feminine grace.

The principal, indeed perhaps the only, sign of advanced old age which the poet presented until near his end was the weakness of his voice. This must have once been, I think, very melodious, but already when I knew him first it had become so faint as to be sometimes scarcely audible, particularly in company. It was therefore most pleasant to be alone with him, especially in the open air, where he seemed to speak with particular freedom and ease. The astonishing fullness of his memory made his conversation marvellous and delightful. He not merely passed, with complete comprehension of the relative distance, from events of 1820 to events of to-day, but his verbal memory was astounding. He garnished his recollections of Wordsworth, Rogers, Landor, or Sir Henry Taylor with copious and repeated quotations from their poetry. Indeed, he once assured me that of certain favourite poets—in particular Wordsworth, Shelley, and Keats—he still retained, at the age of eighty-four, "substantially the bulk of their writings." He said that his principal occupation had been and still was, in his solitary walks or by the fire, to repeat, silently or aloud, pages after pages of poetry. His memory of the great writers was, he believed, so exact that in these exercises he had the illusion that he was reading from the printed book.

The friends of Mr. Aubrey de Vere were so well versed in the stores of his memory that they anticipated an immense pleasure from his "Recollections," which he published in 1897. This was a charming book in many ways, but it was in some degree a disappointment. It was in no sense what we had hoped it would be, an autobiography; it recalled a variety of incidents and places which had interested the writer, yet it told but little of what had moved him most. The inherent delicacy and shyness of the author spoiled the effect. "Self," he said, "is a dangerous personage to let into one's book," but, unfortunately, without it an autobiography is "Hamlet" with the part of the Prince of Denmark omitted. There is much in Aubrey de Vere's "Recollections" which is delightful, but those who enjoyed his conversation miss in the published book a great deal that they recall as particularly original and delightful. For instance, I once asked Mr. de Vere who, among all the great souls he had known, had impressed him the most. He said instantly, "Wordsworth and Newman; they are the two for whom my love has been most like idolatry." There were precious pages about Newman in the "Recollections," but the great disappointment of that book was the comparative absence of any salient notes about Wordsworth. I think Mr. de Vere felt the subject too sacred for public annotation, and yet in personal talk he was always ready to return to it. His loyalty to Wordsworth was a passion. In the very latest letter which I received from him, in a hand so flickering that it is hard to decipher, he says: "Old Christopher North was the first, except Leigh Hunt, who plucked up heart of grace, 'wrote all like a man,' and so forced the public at last to read Wordsworth. He said so often and so loudly—what St. Augustine had said to the pagan world—'So read these things that you may deserve to understand them,' that at last a large part of that world did come to understand that the greatest of the philosophic poets was even then living in their midst." Is it not an enviable gift still to be able to care so much about poetry and philosophy as the ninetieth year approaches?

Many notes which his friends had taken of Mr. de Vere's conversations were rendered nugatory by the publication of his book; some, however, have still their value. He toned down in publication, for instance, the impression of his seeing Newman for the first time in 1838, and his spoken words, which I noted in 1896, were much more vivid. I had asked him to tell me how the future cardinal struck him. He was silent for a moment and then replied, with a light in his blue eyes, " The emotion of seeing him for the first time was one of the greatest in my life. I shall never forget his appearance. I had been waiting some time and then the door opened and Newman, in cap and gown, entered very swiftly and quietly, with a kind of balance of the figure like a very great lady sweeping into the room. That was my first impression ; the second was of a high-bred young monk of the Middle Ages whose asceticism cannot quite conceal his distinguished elegance." Another unpublished impression of Oxford deserves to be recorded. Mr. de Vere went to hear Newman preach his famous sermon on Vain Works. He was a little late, and as he took a remote seat he thought with annoyance that he should not hear anything. But he heard every syllable ; Newman's voice was musical, but very low, yet every word told. Mr. de Vere observed to himself on this occasion that it seemed as though Newman's *thought* was so clear that it was impossible not to perceive the impression of it. You seemed less to be hearing him speak than think. Innumerable links, such as these, with the past were broken by the death of this beloved and venerated man.

A FIRST SIGHT OF
TENNYSON

A FIRST SIGHT OF TENNYSON

THERE is a reaction in the popular feeling about Tennyson, and I am told that upon the young he has lost his hold, which was like that of an octopus upon us in my salad days. These revolutions in taste do not trouble me much; they are inevitable and they are not final. But those who "cannot read" "Maud" and "In Memoriam" to-day must take it on the word of a veteran that forty years ago we, equally, could not help reading them. There was a revolt against the tyranny now and then; in particular, after "The Loves of the Wrens" and 'Enoch Arden" a rather serious mutiny broke out among Tennyson's admirers, but "Lucretius" appeared and they were enslaved again.

It is strange to look back upon the unrestrained panegyric which took the place of the higher criticism of Tennyson in the closing years of the nineteenth century. When a very clever man like the late Duke of Argyll, a man of sober years, could say, without being reproached, that Tennyson's blank verse in the "Idylls" was sweeter and stronger than "the stately march of Elizabethan English in its golden prime";

when Mr. Gladstone could declare of Arthur in the same "Idylls" that he "knew not where to look in history or letters for a nobler or more overpowering conception of man as he might be," then a reaction, however tenderly delayed, was inevitable. The uncritical note of praise is almost more surely hurtful to a reputation than the uncritical note of blame, for it makes a wound that it is much harder to heal. Tennyson is now suffering from the extravagant obsequiousness of his late Victorian admirers. At the moment of which I am about to speak, Tennyson had published nothing since "The Holy Grail," and it was understood that he was slightly startled by the arrival of Swinburne, Morris, and the Rossettis on a stage which he, with Robert Browning still very much in the background, had hitherto sufficiently filled. But the vogue of these new-comers was confined to the elect. In the world at large Tennyson was the English living poet *par excellence*, great by land and great by sea, the one survivor of the heroic chain of masters.

It was the early summer of 1871, and I was palely baking, like a crumpet, in a singularly horrible underground cage, made of steel bars, called the Den. This was a place such as no responsible being is allowed to live in nowadays, where the transcribers on the British Museum staff were immured in a half-light. This cellar was prominently brought forward a year or two later in the course of a Royal Commission on the British Museum, being "lifted into notice" only to be absolutely condemned by the indignation of the medical faculty. I was dolefully engaged here, being then one of the humblest of mankind, a Junior Assistant in the Printed Books Department of the British Museum, on some squalid task, in what was afterwards described by a witness as an atmosphere "scented with rotten morocco, and an indescribable odour familiar in foreign barracks," when a Senior Assistant, one of the rare just spirits in that academical Dotheboys Hall, W. R. S. Ralston, came dashing down the flights of curling steel staircase, to the danger of his six feet six of height, and of the beard that waved down to his waist. Over me he bent, and in a whisper (we were forbidden to speak out loud in the Den) he said, " Come up stairs at once and be presented to Mr. Tennyson ! "

Proud young spirits of the present day, for whom life opens in adulation, will find it scarcely possible to realise what such a summons meant to me. As we climbed those steep and spiral staircases towards light and day, my heart pounded in my chest with agitation. The feeling of excitement was almost overwhelming: it was not peculiar to myself; such ardours were common in those years. Some day a philosopher must analyse it—that enthusiasm of the seventies, that intoxicating belief in "the might of poesy." Tennyson was scarcely a human being to us, he was the God of the Golden Bow; I approached him now like a blank idiot about to be slain, " or was I a worm, too low-crawling for death,

O Delphic Apollo?" It is not merely that no person living now calls forth that kind of devotion, but the sentiment of mystery has disappeared. Not genius itself could survive the kodak snapshots and the halfpenny newspapers.

It must, I suppose, have been one of those days on which the public was then excluded, since we found Tennyson, with a single companion, alone in what was then the long First Sculpture Gallery. His friend was James Spedding, at whom in other conditions I should have gazed with interest, but in the Delphic presence he was not visible to my dazzled eyes. Mr. Thornycroft's statue of the poet, now placed in Trinity College, gives an admirable impression of him at a slightly later date than 1871, if (that is) it is translated out of terms of white into terms of black. Tennyson, at that time, was still one of the darkest of men, as he is familiarly seen in all his earlier portraits. But those portraits do not give, although Mr. Thornycroft has suggested, the singular majesty of his figure, standing in repose. Ralston, for all his six feet six, seemed to dwindle before this magnificent presence, while Tennyson stood, bare-headed among the Roman Emperors, every inch as imperial-looking as the best of them. He stood there as we approached him, very still, with slightly drooping eyelids, and made no movement, no gesture of approach. When I had been presented, and had shaken his hand, he continued to consider me in a silence which would have been deeply disconcerting if it had not, somehow, seemed kindly, and even, absurd as it sounds, rather shy.

The stillness was broken by Ralston's irrelevantly mentioning that I was presently to start for Norway. The bard then began to talk about that country, which I was surprised to find he had visited some dozen years before. Ralston kindly engaged Spedding in conversation, so that Tennyson might now apply himself to me; with infinite goodness he did so, even " making conversation," for I was hopelessly tongue-tied, and must, in fact, have cut a very poor figure. Tennyson, it miraculously appeared, had read some of my stammering verses, and was vaguely gracious about them. He seemed to accept me as a sheep in the fold of which he was, so magnificently, the shepherd. This completed my undoing, but he did not demand from me speech. He returned to the subject of Norway, and said it was not the country for him to travel in, since you could only travel in it in funny little round carts, called *karjols*, which you must drive yourself, and that he was far too near-sighted for that. (I had instantly wondered at his double glasses, of a kind I had never seen before.)

Then somebody suggested that we should examine the works of art, which, in that solitude, we could delightfully do. Tennyson led us, and we stopped at any sculpture which attracted his notice. But the only remark which my memory has retained was made before the famous black bust of Antinous. Tennyson bent forward a little, and said, in his deep, slow voice, "Ah! this is the inscrutable Bithynian!" There was a pause, and then he added, gazing into the eyes of the bust: "If we knew what he knew, we should understand the ancient world." If I live to be a hundred years old, I shall still hear his rich tones as he said this, without emphasis, without affectation, as though he were speaking to himself. And soon after, the gates of heaven were closed, and I went down three flights of stairs to my hell of rotten morocco.

A VISIT TO WHITTIER

A VISIT TO WHITTIER

WHEN I was in Boston in 1884, my brilliant and hospitable friend Mr. W. D. Howells received a letter from the poet Whittier, expressing a most kind wish that I should visit him. It would have been a great satisfaction to me to have seen him in summer, and in his own beautiful home at Amesbury, where he settled in 1836, and where he resided until his death in 1892, although at the moment of his demise he happened to be visiting a friend at Horton Falls. It would have been delightful to carry away an impression of that noble, calm figure in the midst of its household gods. But, if I remember rightly, the mansion at Amesbury was at that time being altered in some way; at all events, Mr. Whittier was staying with female relations at a house, called Oak Knoll, near the town of Danvers. It was, moreover, in the depth of the hard New England winter; all the landscape was choked with snow. Certainly, the visitor's attention would be the more exclusively concentrated on the appearance and conversation of his celebrated host. Accordingly, an appointment was made, and on December 6 I set forth on quite an arctic expedition to discover the author of "Snow Bound."

I have a superstition that all very agreeable adventures begin with a slight mishap. I was not prepared to believe Mr. Whittier so difficult to reach as I found him. We arrived early at the dismal railway station of Danvers, and a hack was persuaded to drive us to the entrance of Oak Knoll. All this Massachusetts landscape, doubtless enchanting at other times of the year, is of a most forbidding bleakness in midwinter. The carriage deposited us and drove off, leaving us to struggle up to the homestead, and we arrived with relief under the great pillars of an ample piazza. Perhaps, in leafy seasons, Oak Knoll may have its charms, but it was distinctly sinister that December morning.

We rang, and after a long pause the front door opened slightly, and a very unprepossessing dog emerged, and shut the door (if I may say so) behind him. We were face to face with this animal, which presented none of the features identified in one's mind with the idea of Mr. Whittier. It sniffed unpleasantly, but we spoke to it most blandly, and it became assured that we were not tramps. The dog sat down and looked at us; we had nowhere to sit down, but we looked at the dog. Then, after many blandishments, but feeling very uncomfortable, I ventured to hold the dog in conversation, while I rang again. After another pause, the door was very slightly opened, and a voice of no agreeable timbre asked what we wanted. We explained, across the dog, that we had come by appointment to see Mr. Whittier. The door was closed a second time, and, if our carriage had still been waiting, we should certainly have driven back to Danvers. But at length a hard-featured woman grudgingly admitted us, and showed us, growling as she did it, into a parlour.

Our troubles were then over, for Mr. Whittier himself appeared, with all that report had ever told of gentle sweetness and dignified, cordial courtesy. He was then seventy-seven years old, and, although he spoke of age and feebleness, he showed few signs of either ; he was, in fact, to live eight years more. Perhaps because the room was low, he seemed surprisingly tall ; he must, in fact, have been a little less than six feet high. The peculiarity of his face rested in the extraordinarily large and luminous black eyes, set in black eyebrows, and fringed with thick black eyelashes curiously curved inwards. This bar of vivid black across the countenance was startlingly contrasted with the bushy snow-white beard and hair, offering a sort of contradiction which was surprising and presently pleasing. He was careful to keep on my right side, I noticed, being presumably deaf in the right ear ; even if this were the case, which he concealed, his hearing continued to be markedly quick in a man of his years.

His generosity to those much younger and less gifted than himself is well known, and I shall not dwell on the good-natured things which he proceeded to say to his English visitor. He made no profession at any time of being a critic, and his formula was that such and such verse or prose had given him pleasure—"I am grateful to thee for all that enjoyment," was his charming way of being kind. But I will mention what he said about one book, the "Life of Gray," because I do not remember that Gray is mentioned in any of the published works of Whittier. He said that he had delighted in that narrative of a life so quiet and so sequestered that, as he put it, it was almost more "Quakerly" than that of any famous member of the Society; and he added that he had been greatly moved by the fullness and the significance of a career which to the outside world might have seemed absolutely without movement. "Thee were very fortunate," he went on, "to have that beautiful, restful story left to tell after almost all the histories of great men had been made so fully known to readers."

He asked me what and whom I had seen. Had I yet visited Concord? I responded that I was immediately about to do so, and then he said quickly, "Ah! thee should have come a little sooner, when we were still united. There were four of us a little while ago, but two are gone, and what is Concord without Emerson?" He spoke with great emotion of Emerson—"the noblest human being I have known"—and of Longfellow—"perhaps the sweetest. But you will see Holmes," he added. I replied it was my great privilege to be seeing Dr. Holmes every day, and that the night before he had sent all sorts of affectionate messages

A Visit to Whittier

by me to Mr. Whittier. The latter expressed great curiosity to see Holmes's short "Life of Emerson," which, in fact, was published five or six days later. With reminiscences of the past, and especially of the great group of the poets his contemporaries, my venerable host kept me long entertained.

He presently said that he would leave me that he might search for a portrait of himself, which he was so kind as to offer to me as a memorial of my visit. I proposed to take my leave, but he insisted that I must not go; he was absent about twenty minutes, resting, as I gathered, from the exertion of speaking, which had caused a noticeable hoarseness. He returned, entirely refreshed, and was once more delightfully communicative. I know not how he was induced to go back to the early anti-slavery days, but this subject having been started, he pursued it with the greatest vivacity. I was left with the impression that on his sedentary and noiseless existence the troubles of 1835 had left an indelible impression—that these formed, indeed, the most exciting pivot for his reminiscences. He told the story of the Concord riots eagerly and merrily, no doubt in almost the same words as he had often told it before. His eyes flashed, he slapped his knees, he may almost be said to have gesticulated, and there was something less than Quakerly quietism in his gusto at the exciting incidents of the narrative. He told how he was met in the street of Concord by the rioters, who were looking for George Thompson, the abolitionist lecturer.

Thompson was a man of about his own age, and the mob, supposing Whittier to be he, pelted the poet with rotten eggs and, worse than that, with stones. Their aim was bad, for they scarcely touched Whittier with the more serious missiles, which rattled instead on the wooden fence behind him. He said it made him feel like the Apostle Paul. Another abolitionist, a Mr. Kent, at this moment providentially opened his street-door, and Whittier was pulled in out of the angry crowd. I forget exactly what happened next, but there was a great deal of shouting and firing, and in the process of time George Thompson seems to have joined the other anti-slavery men in their refuge. At all events, Mr. Whittier described, with immense animation and spirit, how it became necessary at length to make a dash, and how Thompson and he were brought in a carriage to a side-door, and the horse suddenly whipped through the unexpectant crowds out of the town and far away before any one thought of pursuing them. At this final recital the old gentleman could remain seated no longer, but started from his chair and fought his battle o'er again. No doubt it was all recorded history, and could be reconstructed with closer accuracy from the books, but it was a delightful and quite sufficing experience to hear it thus told by the most distinguished person engaged, after an interim of nearly fifty years.

If it is not too trifling, I must mention, in connection with his magnificent, lustrous eyes, that, the conversation turning upon the hues of things, Mr. Whittier greatly surprised me by confessing that he was quite colour-blind. He exemplified his condition by saying that if I came to Amesbury I should be scandalised by one of his carpets. It appeared that he was never permitted by the guardian goddesses of his hearth to go "shopping" for himself, but that once, being in Boston, and remembering that he needed a carpet, he had ventured to go to a store and buy what he thought to be a very nice, quiet article, precisely suited to adorn a Quaker home. When it arrived at Amesbury there was a universal shout of horror, for what had struck Mr. Whittier as a particularly soft combination of browns and greys proved to normal eyes to be a loud pattern of bright red roses on a field of the crudest cabbage-green. When he had told me this, it was then easy to observe that the fullness and brilliancy of his wonderful eyes had something which was not entirely normal about them.

He struck me as very gay and cheerful, in spite of his occasional references to the passage of time and the vanishing of beloved faces. He even laughed, frequently and with a childlike suddenness, but without a sound. His face had none of the immobility so frequent with very aged persons; on the contrary, waves of mood were always sparkling across his features and leaving nothing stationary there except the narrow, high, and strangely receding forehead. His language, very fluid and easy, had an agreeable touch of the soil, an occasional rustic note in its elegant colloquialism, that seemed very pleasant and appropriate, as if it linked him naturally with the long line of sturdy ancestors of whom he was the final blossoming. In connection with his poetry, I think it would be difficult to form in the imagination a figure more appropriate to Whittier's writings than Whittier himself proved to be in the flesh.

Two days later I received from Mr. Whittier a very kind letter and the gift of his latest volume of poems, "The Bay of Seven Islands." It was far from being his last, for it was to be followed by two more in his lifetime and by a gleaning of posthumous verses. But it was the book of an old man, and in reading it one was reminded that fifty-three years had passed since "Legends of New England" had first given the name of Whittier to the lovers of poetry. In saying that "The Bay of Seven Islands" is an old man's book, however, I do not mean that it shows marks of senile failure, but only that the eye of the writer is constantly on the past, counting the sheaves, watching the red colour in the western sky. In verses not less sincere because they are a little rough, he offers his own apologia. He desires, he says, that it shall be said of him when he is gone:

> *Hater of din and riot*
> *He lived in days unquiet;*
> *And, lover of all beauty,*
> *Trod the hard ways of duty.*

To all who dumbly suffered,
His tongue and pen he offered;
His life was not his own,
Nor lived for self alone.

This we can clearly assert must always be said of Whittier. But what will impartial criticism, which is deaf to all the virtues if their expression be not enshrined and kept fresh in really fine literature, decide about the poetry of this good and graceful man?

Mr. Whittier was composing verses all his life, and the difference of quality between those he wrote at twenty and at eighty is remarkably small. He was a poet in the lifetime of Gifford and Crabbe, and he was still a poet when Mr. Rudyard Kipling was already famous. During this vast period of time his style changed very little; it had its ups and downs, its laxities and then its felicities, but it bore very little relation to passing conditions. There rose up beside it Tennyson and Browning, Rossetti and Swinburne, but none of these affected Whittier. His genius, or talent, or knack—whichever we choose to call it—was an absolutely local and native thing. It was like the Indian waters of strange name of which it sang, Winnepesaukee and Merrimac and Katahdin; it streamed forth, untouched by Europe, from among the butternuts and maples of the hard New England landscape. The art in Whittier's verse was primitive. Those who love his poetry most will wish that he had possessed a better ear, that he could have felt that "mateless" does not rhyme with "greatness." In all his books there is a tendency to excess, to

K

redundancy; he babbles on, even when he has nothing very inspired to say.

But when all this is acknowledged, none but a very hasty reader will fail to recognise Whittier's lasting place in the history of literature. He is not rich, nor sonorous, nor a splendid artist; he is even rather rarely exquisite, but he has an individuality of his own that is of durable importance. He is filled with moral enthusiasm, as a trumpet is filled with the breath of him who blows it. His Quaker quietism concentrates itself till it breaks in a real passion-storm of humanity, and when Whittier is roused he sings with the thrilling sweetness of a wood-thrush. By dint of simplicity and earnestness, he frequently hits upon the most charming phrases, instinct with life and truth; so that the English poet with whom it seems most natural to compare him in the lyrical order is the epic and didactic Crabbe. If the author of "The Borough" had been dowered with the gift of writing in octosyllabics and short stanzaic measures, and had been born of stern Puritan stock in Massachusetts, and had been roused by the sight of a public iniquity, such as slavery, recognised and applauded in society, he might have presented to the world a talent very much resembling that of Whittier. But, as it is, we look around in vain for an English or American poet of anything like the same merit who shares the place of Whittier.

The grave of the admirable Quaker poet at Amesbury is hemmed in by a hedge of vigorous arbor vitæ. His memory, in like manner, depends for its protection, not on the praise of exotic communities which can never, though they admire, rightly comprehend it, but on the conscience of New England, shy, tenacious, intrepid, to which, more than any other poet has done, Whittier made a direct and constant appeal.

THE AUTHOR OF "JOHN INGLESANT"
1834–1903

THE AUTHOR OF "JOHN INGLESANT"

THE two volumes of her husband's "Letters and Literary Remains," which Mrs. Shorthouse published in 1905, must have familiarised a great number of readers with a favourite author who, during his lifetime, was something of a mystery to most of them. In order to see Joseph Henry Shorthouse in the flesh it was necessary to make a pilgrimage to Birmingham, where he shone for twenty years as the principal literary light. Over this light, even in its provincial sphere, for a long time there descended more and more closely the extinguisher of an ill-health which gradually obscured it completely. One cannot be certain that even these volumes, so devotedly and so punctiliously prepared by his widow, will repeat for the many the impression which his very curious person made upon the few who knew him. Upon myself, who saw him first nearly thirty years ago, when his energies were at their height, the effect he then made was startling. I had vaguely anticipated something Quakerish or clerical, something faintly recalling the seventeenth-century Puritan clergyman, with perhaps a touch of Little Gidding. Very elegant and colourless, one fancied him; a grave man, pale with meditation and dyed in the drab tincture of provinciality.

The exact opposite was the fact. J. H. Shorthouse was one of the most eighteenth-century-looking people who have been seen in our day. But it was not the eighteenth century of Gainsborough and Romney which he represented; it was Italian. To tell the truth, the instant and irresistible impression which he gave was that of a mask of 1750 suddenly revived out of some serious and romantic pastoral. He did not seem a part of actual existence; he made his entry *facendo il bergamasco,* and one almost expected him to take off his large artificial face, so much too big for his body, and reveal a living Shorthouse below. With this curious illusion of wearing a mask were connected his love of a discreet but unusual gaiety of colour in dress, and the movements of his soft, slightly prelatical hands. His extreme courtesy and his few and stereotyped but unusual gestures made it easy to think of a Shorthouse, scarcely changed at all, moving in the kaleidoscopic procession of figures in some Neapolitan festival. Mrs. Shorthouse, with laudable courage, does not attempt to disguise from her readers what was the great physical misfortune of her husband's life, his incurable stammer. When I knew him first, this was not yet incessant and was still under some control. But it added to that strange resemblance with Italian types of the eighteenth century, since the recollection of the stutter of Tartaglia (if I may be pardoned for saying so) was made irresistible by it.

It is perhaps not fantastic to say that, in his intellectual character also, Shorthouse loved to wear a domino and fling a purple cloak across his shoulders. His mind went through life playing a grave and graceful part, and his whole scheme of culture was a delicate sport or elaborate system of make-believe. He had never been in Italy, or, indeed, across the English Channel, yet he loved to fancy that he had travelled extensively and confidentially in romantic Catholic countries. It is the custom nowadays to speak of his pictures of Italy as artless and "clumsy"—the word (which would have cut Shorthouse to the quick) was actually used to describe them the other day. It does not seem to me that they deserve this censure, which is based upon a supposition that every author is bound to paint topographically, with his eye on the object, like Ruskin or Mr. Maurice Hewlett. Some people think they have swept Shorthouse away if they can prove that a palace which he supposed to be of white marble is really built of red brick. The staircase of the house in Edgbaston was lined with fine impressions of the engravings of Piranesi, and Shorthouse, seeing my eye rest on these one day, said, "I got all my Italian local colour out of those prints." Now, it is—not to be captious—precisely "colour" that one does not get out of the stately convention of Piranesi. Consequently, the author of "John Inglesant" had, unconsciously, to supply a great deal out of his brooding imagination. The whole thing was false, in a sense, if you like to put it so; he was not describing, he was hardly creating, he was simply *facendo il bergamasco*.

The author who "does his bergamask" runs the greatest risk of being misconceived by criticism. All the righteous commonplaces are trotted out against him. He is told that what he writes is laboured and unreal, he is called self-conscious and academic, he is advised to put off his domino and his cloak and to behave like other people. He is reproved because life does not affect him directly and because he has no objective sympathy with mankind. This is the note of clever criticism to-day with regard to "John Inglesant," a book which seems to have passed, perhaps only for the moment, out of fashion. The way to meet these attacks, it seems to me, is to admit their premises, and then to inquire what it all matters. If we are to accept only one kind of fiction, strong in humour, vivid and strenuous in relation to life, standing sturdily on two sound legs of common-sense, then we must confine ourselves to a very few books, of which "Tom Jones" is unquestionably the best. But without withdrawing a single epithet of eulogy from Fielding and the great realists, we must consent to widen our borders sufficiently to embrace the fantastic, the unreal, the capricious types of fiction. The terms which are used nowadays to exclude "John Inglesant" from commendation would forbid us to admire "La Princesse de Clèves" on the one hand and "The Shaving of Shagpat" on the other. This is a tendency which must be resisted. There is a legitimate pleasure to be found in the cultivation of a moral spectacle. It was this, a sort of *commedia erudita*, which it was Shorthouse's aim to produce. He did so in "John Inglesant," and more exquisitely still, it seems to me, in a book which has never been properly appreciated, "The Little Schoolmaster Mark."

There are certain points of view from which these romances must always retain their importance for the social student of the mid-Victorian period. They are the typical novels of the great awakening of middle-class culture in the sixties. In those days Oxford might possess its Matthew Arnold, and Chelsea its Whistler, and Fairyland its Rossetti and its Morris, but it was inconceivable that Birmingham could exhibit a school of beauty or a cult of romance. The extraordinary success of "John Inglesant" resulted from its answer to the appeal for new light from the Midlands, to the cry from local centres which still lay in æsthetic darkness, but had heard that the dayspring of art was at hand. Shorthouse, who liked to talk about his books with his intimate friends, often spoke to me about the inception of "John Inglesant." He regarded it, I think, as a little mysterious, almost supernatural. He did not fatuously exaggerate the importance of it, but it was impossible for him to ignore the tremendous response which came back to him from its readers. He was a little alarmed, immensely pleased, and most of all surprised. As he talked of the career of the novel, his large solemn face, with its incredible whiskers, would take an air of almost pathetic astonishment.

His attitude was, so far as sobriety would allow him to suggest it, that "John Inglesant" was the result of a kind of vocation. He was without pride, but he really believed that the subject was "given" to him, and he was wont to quote of himself, as a writer, "Blessed is the man whom Thou choosest, and causest to approach unto Thee, that he may dwell in Thy courts." In 1866 he began to feel that he must write a book—he, a shy, Quakerish manufacturer, without literary training, subdued by persistent ill-health. Nobody suggested or encouraged this idea, but it grew; "if it were only quite a little book which nobody read, I should like to write one." Then, as he brooded vaguely, he read a paragraph somewhere about a knight who forgave the murderer of his brother. This was the grain of mustard-seed, and it took ten years for it to bourgeon into the great Christian romance we all know. Meantime, the simplicity of Shorthouse's intellectual life must have been something extraordinary. He became acquainted—this alone shows the vacancy of the world in which he had lived—about the age of thirty-two, he became acquainted with "The Christian Year" and the poems of Wordsworth. The visit of a "venerable and beloved" bishop to Birmingham filled him with enthusiasm ; his lordship came to tea, consented to read some passages of Wordsworth aloud in the Shorthouses' drawing-room, and was let into the secret that his host had " written a book." The bishop read it, and said that it "contains a great deal of very unusual information." Another bishop, equally affable, went further, and said that he did not know whether he had " ever read a book of the kind which had struck or interested him more." We seem walking among shadows in these faint emotions, and in the centre is a half-bewildered Shorthouse, with rapturous face upturned, aghast at the prescience of these prelates. But when had a famous book a stranger birth ?

"John Inglesant" was privately printed—for no publisher would take the risk of it—in 1880. Shorthouse was in his forty-seventh year, and expected nothing more of life, save perhaps richer vestmented services at church on Sundays, a fresh talk over the tea-table with some visiting bishop, and a shy communication by letter, now and then, with some author unknown to him whose works had delighted him. But all through these years, in reality, he had been insensibly growing into his own type ; he had fixed his eyes on a moderate antiquity until he had begun to be moderately antique himself. He began to inhabit Edgbaston, that serene and highly cultured apanage to Birmingham, breathlessly, as if it were the gate of Heaven. At length he was actually summoned to London to breakfast with Mr. Gladstone (May 4, 1882), and he went, dreadfully alarmed, but believing it to be his æsthetic privilege and duty to obey, much as St. Francis might have left Assisi for Rome. And this was the occasion, I think, on which he finally adopted his bergamask. He was no longer Mr. Joseph Henry Shorthouse, the vitriol manufacturer of Birmingham; he was the author of "John Inglesant," into whose earthen vessel had been divinely poured waters for the healing of the nations.

Lest I be misunderstood to speak slightingly, in trying to speak carefully, of this excellent man, whom I admired and loved, I would immediately proceed to say what in his own idea justified the slightly solemn way in which he regarded his mission. He believed that he had been raised up to persuade people that God prefers culture to fanaticism. He asserted this again and again; the formula is his own. He disliked excess of every kind—tumultuous benevolence, exaggerated faith, fanatical action. He was of opinion that our English life, public and private, as it was worked out to a practical issue forty years ago, was a mistake. He was an epicurean quietist, who believed that the main object of every man's life should be to conquer and secure for himself peace of mind and a solution of the intellectual difficulties which have perplexed him. He held that so far as philanthropy, or active energy of any sort, was incompatible with perfect culture, it was wrong, it was unwholesome and immoral. In his attitude towards altruism and public pity, the author of "John Inglesant," arriving from the opposite point of the compass, was oddly in harmony with Nietzsche, of whom he had never heard, and whom he would have looked upon as a ruffian. Shorthouse grew, gentle as he was, quite courageous when the ideas in "John Inglesant" were attacked. Lord Acton found fault with the character of the Jesuit; Shorthouse replied, " I never reason with Roman Catholics: they live in a fairyland of their own "—a delightful rejoinder.

The success of "John Inglesant" occurred thirty years ago, and the world has a short memory. But some of us, alas! can very clearly recall the momentous circumstances of it. Mr. Gladstone, swept away by the tide of enthusiasm, yet ambitious to guide it, was photographed with the second volume of "John Inglesant" open on his knee, "the title of the book quite plain" even to those outside the shop-windows of the vendors. Not provincial prelates any longer, but archbishops, cardinals, professors, ladies of the first quality bombarded Edgbaston with their correspondence. For the next five years, at least, Shorthouse was an accepted celebrity, the champion of good taste, the unfailing source of rather vague but always stimulating "thoughts about beauty," the introducer into middle-class life and conduct of an extreme refinement. It was much to his advantage, and, perhaps, a proof of his wisdom, that he resisted all incitements to break up his provincial habits and be translated to residence in London. It was in Birmingham, and only in Birmingham, as an unconscious sentiment taught him, that he could carry on his graceful, intellectual parade without disturbance. It depended extremely on exterior symbols and superficial attitudes.

It behoves us to speak with no less respect than sympathy of another phase of Shorthouse's character into the cultivation of which he threw particular care. But in the religious aspect of his genius, too, I find the same remarkable cultivation of external characteristics. Shall we say that when he went to church, as he so consistently loved to do, he still wore the domino? I think we must say so, and certainly he was never more sincere nor more individual than when he dwelt upon the importance of cultivating the religious symbol. In literature, in art, in piety, it was the becoming attitude which Shorthouse valued, not merely for its own sake, but because he believed that it naturally led to sympathy and delicacy, and perhaps—but this was less essential— to faith itself. In the course of my own long talks with him, this preference for ceremony over dogma, this instinct for the beautiful parade and refined self-surrender of religion, grew to seem the central feature of Shorthouse's intellectual character, explaining everything in his books, in his letters, in his personal conduct. He wished, as we know, that the agnostic should be persuaded to come to the Sacrament, not that he might testify to a creed which he did not share, but that "some effect of sympathy, some magic chord and thrill of sweetness should mollify and refresh his heart."

There are, of course, a great many sensible and strong-minded people who object to this whole attitude, who insist that we should be our own plain selves, and wear no mask in literature or in religion. These people would have had Shorthouse remember that he was a manufacturer of vitriol (a quaint fact which, I think, Mrs. Shorthouse never happens to mention), "behaving as such" quite prosaically wherever the wealth of Birmingham was gathered together. But, as the poet pathetically puts it, "the world is full of a number of things," and oceans of sulphuric acid will be poured out before we have another visionary dreamer like the author of " John Inglesant." His sequestered existence, which would have made him earth-bound if he had not lifted himself on the wings of fancy, concentrated his peculiarities and intensified a sort of exquisite provinciality. Shorthouse was very modest, with a due self-consciousness of merit ; he was very simple, with a certain love of pomp and artifice ; he clung to a sense of the importance of beauty as a safeguard against what was small and tiresome in daily life. It would be an exaggeration to put Shorthouse in the forefront of the authors of the nineteenth century. His work is not copious enough and not spontaneous enough for that. But he had a real talent for carefully studied and delicately harmonious prose, and for that kind of painstaking literary harlequinade which we call *pastiche*.

It is customary to say that the present generation has forgotten Shorthouse. If that is true, let it be reminded of his admirable characteristics by the pious labours of his widow. But I think we are apt to judge too hastily of what "the younger generation" is supposed to remember or to forget. The impress of Shorthouse's genius seems to me, on the contrary, to be patent on many sides of us. We see it, surely, in recent books so dissimilar and yet so admirable as "Ariadne in Mantua" and "Zuleika Dobson." The bergamot perfume persists; it would be absurd to wish that it should pervade every bouquet. But we must hope that "the younger generation," that mysterious band of invaders, will deign to read the volumes of essays and letters which Mrs. Shorthouse presented to them. They will find, I admit, a certain faintness, a certain weakness and ineffectuality, but it will be astonishing if they do not also admit that "an inexpressibly sweet and delicate melody has penetrated their senses."

MANDELL CREIGHTON
1843–1901

MANDELL CREIGHTON

IN heroic times, when a monarch was about to make a solemn adventure into strange dominions, he chose one of the wisest and noblest of his subjects, and sent him forward as a herald. Those who indulge such fancies may have seen a mysterious revival of this custom in the fate which removed the admirable Bishop of London exactly eight days before his Queen was called upon to take the same dread journey. If ceremonial had demanded, at the approach of such an event, a sacrifice of the most honoured, the most valued, the most indispensable, many alternatives would have occurred to those on whom the wretched duty of choice would have fallen; but it is probable that among the first half-dozen of such precious names would have been found that of a Churchman, Mandell Creighton. His wholesome virtues, his indefatigable vigour, the breadth of his sympathy, the strenuous activity of his intellect, pointed him out as the man who more than any other seemed destined to justify the ways of the national Church in the eyes of modern thought, the ecclesiastic who more than any other would continue to conciliate the best and keenest secular opinion.

In Creighton, in short, a real prince of the Church seemed to be approaching the ripeness of his strength. He seemed preparing to spend the next quarter of a century in leading a huge and motley flock more or less safely into tolerably green pastures. Here, then, we thought we had found, what we so rarely see in England, a political prelate of the first rank. With all this were combined gifts of a literary and philosophical order, a lambent wit, a nature than which few have been known more generous or affectionate, and a constitution which promised to defy the years. No wonder, then, if Creighton had begun to take his place as one of the most secure and precious of contemporary institutions. In the fullness of his force, at the height of his intellectual meridian, he suddenly dropped out of the sky. And with all the sorrow that we felt was mingled the homely poignancy of a keen disappointment.

I

Mandell Creighton was the son of Robert Creighton, timber merchant of Carlisle, and of Sarah Mandell, his wife. On both sides he came of sound Cumberland stock. He was born at Carlisle, on July 5, 1843. He went to school at Durham, and in 1862 he was elected "postmaster" of Merton College, Oxford; that is to say, a scholar supported on the foundation. He spent the next thirteen years at the university; and this period forms one of the most important of the sharply marked stages into which Creighton's life was divided. Oxford, Embleton, Cambridge, Peterborough, London—it is very seldom that the career of a modern man is subdivided by such clean sword-cuts through the texture of his personal habits. But it was the earliest of these stages which really decided the order and character of the others. It is easy to think of a Creighton who was never Bishop of Peterborough; it is already becoming difficult to recollect at all clearly the one who was Dixie Professor at Cambridge. But to think of Creighton and not think of Oxford is impossible. From the beginning of his career to the close of it he exhaled the spirit of that university.

Those who knew Creighton as Bishop of London may feel that they knew him as a young tutor at Oxford. Those whose friendship with him goes back further than mine tell me that as quite a young undergraduate he had exactly the same manner which we became accustomed to later. He never changed in the least essential matter; he grew in knowledge and experience, indeed, but the character was strongly sketched in him from the very first. Boys are quick in their instinctive observation, and almost as a freshman Creighton was dubbed "the Professor." At Merton they were fond of nicknames, and they liked them short; it followed that the future Bishop of London, during his undergraduate days, was known among his intimates as "the P." He wore glasses, and they gleamed already with something of the flash that was to become so famous. In those earliest days, when other boys were largely playing the fool, Creighton was instinctively practising to play the teacher. Already, indeed, he was scholastic in the habit of his mind, although never, I think, what could, with even an undergraduate's exaggeration, be styled "priggish." I have heard of the zeal with which, at a very early age, quite secretly and unobtrusively, he would help lame (and presumably idle) dogs over educational stiles. He was not a cricketer, but he took plenty of strenuous exercise in the form of walking and rowing. He sought glory in the Merton boat, and it is still remembered that he was an ornament to a certain nautical club, composed of graduates, and called the Ancient Mariners. But the maniacal lovers of athletic exercise can never quote Creighton as one of their examples.

When he became a don—fellow and tutor of his college—the real life of Creighton began. The chrysalis broke, and the academic butterfly appeared. With a certain small class of men at Merton he was, I believe, for a very short time, unpopular. It was a college illustrious for the self-abandonment of high spirits, and Creighton had a genius for discipline. But he was very soon respected, and his influence over each of his particular pupils was tremendous. It is interesting to note that while everybody speaks of Creighton's "influence" over himself or others, no one ever seems to recall any "influence" from without acting upon Creighton. As to the undergraduates brought under his care from 1866 onwards, there is probably not one surviving who does not recollect the young tutor with respect, and few who do not look back upon him with affection. As a disciplinarian he was quick and firm; he was no martinet, but the men under his charge soon understood that they must work hard and behave themselves. From each he would see that he got the best there was to give.

He had great courage; it was always one of his qualities. One of the most remarkable exhibitions of it, I think, was his custom—while he was a fellow at Merton, and afterwards when he was professor at Cambridge—of holding informal meetings in his rooms, at which he allowed any species of historical conundrum to be put to him, and enforced himself to give a reasonable answer to it. The boys would try to pose him, of course; would grub up out-of-the-way bits of historical erudition. Creighton was always willing "to face the music," and I have never heard of his being drawn into any absurd position. Few pundits of a science would be ready to undergo such a searching test of combined learning and common-sense.

Of Creighton's particular pupils, in those early days, two at least were destined to hold positions of great prominence. In none of the obituary notices of the Bishop of London, so far as I saw, were his interesting relations with Lord Randolph Churchill so much as mentioned. A few months after Creighton was placed on the governing body of Merton, Lord Randolph made his appearance there as an undergraduate. He was conspicuous, in those days, as an unpromising type of the rowdy nobleman. Nobody, not even his own family, believed in a respectable future for him; but Creighton, with that singular perspicacity which was one of his more remarkable characteristics, divined better things in Lord Randolph at once. A friend was once walking with the tutor of Merton, when down the street came swaggering and strutting, with a big nosegay at his buttonhole and a moustache curled skywards, Lord Randolph Churchill, dressed, as they say, "to kill." The friend could not resist a gesture of disdain, but Creighton said: "You are like everybody else: you think he is an awful ass! You are wrong: he isn't. You will see that he will have a brilliant future, and what's more definite, a brilliant political future. See whether my prophecy doesn't turn out true." All through the period of Lord Randolph Churchill's amazing harvest of wild oats Creighton continued to believe in him. I recollect challenging his faith in 1880, when Lord Randolph was covering himself, after his second election for Woodstock, with ridicule. He replied: "You think all this preposterous conduct is mere folly? You are wrong: it is only the fermentation of a very remarkable talent." Of course he was right; and as he lived to rejoice in the rush of his meteor heavenwards, he lived to lament the earthward tumble of all the sparks and sticks. Another undergraduate of eminence, to whose care Creighton was specially appointed, was the Queen's youngest son, Leopold, Duke of Albany, to whom he gave private lessons in history and literature, and over whose mind he exercised a highly beneficial influence. It was Prince Leopold who first introduced Creighton's name to the Queen, and started her interest in his ecclesiastical career.

It was not until he became a don at Merton, in 1866, that Creighton formed a group of really intimate friends. Then, immediately, his talents and his conversation opened to him the whole circle of the best minds of Oxford. No one could be more attractive in such a society. His affectionate nature and his very fresh and vigorous intellect made him the most delightful of companions, and he was preserved by a certain inherent magnanimity from the pettiness which sometimes afflicts university coteries. From the very first it was understood that he would be an historian (although, by the irony of examinations, he had gained only a "second class" in modern history), but it was not clearly seen how this obvious native bent would be made to serve a profession. Suddenly, to everybody's great surprise, in 1870 he was ordained deacon, and priest in 1873. The reasons which led him to take so unexpected a step have been frequently the subject of conjecture. I shall presently, in endeavouring to form a portrait of his character, return to a consideration of this most interesting and important question.

He was now, at the age of thirty, one of the most individual types which Oxford, then abounding in men of character, could offer to the observation of a visitor. He was already one of the features of the society: he was, perhaps, more frequently and freely discussed than any other Oxonian of his years. He was too strong a man to be universally approved of: the dull thought him paradoxical, the solemn thought him flippant; already there was the whisper abroad that he was "not a spiritually-minded man." But the wise and the good, if they sometimes may have doubted his gravity, never doubted his sincerity; nor would there be many ready to denounce their own appreciation of good company by declaring his conversation anything but most attractive.

It was soon after he became a priest—it was in the early summer of 1874—that I first met Creighton. I was on a visit to Walter Pater and his sisters, who were then residing in the suburbs of Oxford, in Bradmore Road. To luncheon on Sunday came a little party of distinguished guests—Henry Smith and his sister, Max Müller, Bonamy Price (I think), and lastly Mr. and Mrs. Creighton; for he had married two years before this. Much the youngest person present, I kept an interested silence; most of the talk, indeed, being fitted for local consumption, and, to one who knew little of Oxford, scarcely intelligible. During the course of the meal, at which Creighton scintillated with easy mastery, I caught his hawk's eye fall upon me once or twice; and when it was over, and the ladies had left us, he quitted his own friends, and coming over to me proposed a walk in the garden. I cannot say that this brilliant clergyman, of doubtful age and intimidating reputation, was quite the companion I should have ventured to choose. But we descended on to the greensward; and as, through that long golden afternoon, we walked up and down the oblong garden, I gave myself more and more unreservedly to the charm of my magnetic companion, to his serious wit and whimsical wisdom, to the directness of his sympathy, and to the firmness of his grasp of the cord of life. I was conscious of an irresistible intuition that this was one of the best as well as one of the most remarkable men whom I was ever likely to meet; and our friendship began in that hour.

II

From the first it seemed inevitable to count Creighton among men of letters, and yet the outward evidence of his literary life was very scanty to the close of his Oxford period. In all his spare time he was preparing for his future work, and perhaps he was already publishing anonymously some of his papers; but the fact remains that his name did not appear on a title-page until he was leaving Oxford, in 1875. I fancy that the difficulty he found in concentrating his attention on literature was one of several reasons which so suddenly took him to Northumberland in that year. He had already begun to plan his *magnum opus*, "The History of the Papacy," but he was struck with the impossibility of combining the proper composition of such a work with the incessant duties of a college tutor. Hence, to most people's intense surprise, it was one day abruptly announced that Creighton had accepted the remote vicarage of Embleton. He had given no one an opportunity of advising him against the step, but it was known that he had strengthened his determination by taking counsel with Henry Smith. That wisest of men had urged upon him the necessity, if he was to enlarge his sphere of activity, and to rise to a really commanding position in the Church, of his seeing the other side of clerical life, the parochial. With the academic side Creighton was sufficiently familiar; what he needed now was the practically pastoral. Those who lamented that he should be snatched from the gardens and classrooms of Oxford, and from their peripatetic ingenuities, had to realise that their charming friend was a very strong man, predestined to do big things, and that the time had come when solitude and fixity were needful for his spiritual development.

So Creighton went off to Embleton; and one remembers the impression among his friends that it was something worse for them, in the way of exile, than Tomi could have been for the companions of Ovid. But there was a great deal to mitigate the horrors of exile. In the first place, Embleton was the best of all the livings in the gift of Merton College, and in many respects delightful, socially as well as physically. The vicarage was a very pleasant house, nested in tall trees, which were all the more precious because of the general bareness and bleakness of the grey Northumbrian landscape. A mile away to the east, broadly ribboned by rolling lion-coloured sands, is the sea—the troubled Euxine of those parts—with a splendid ruin, the keep of Dunstanborough Castle, crouching on a green crag. To the west, dreary flat lands are bounded, towards evening and on clear mornings, by the far-away jags of the Cheviot Hills. On the whole, it is a bright, hard, tonical country, lacking the voluptuous beauties of the south, but full of attraction to a strong and rapid man. It is a land but little praised, although it has had one ardent lover in Mr. Swinburne, that " flower of bright Northumberland," that " sea-bird of the loud sea strand," who sings the strenuous Tale of Balen. It always seemed to me that this landscape, this bleak and austere Northumbrian vigour, exactly suited the genius of Creighton. It made a background to him, at all events ; and if I paint his full-length portrait in my mind's eye, it is always with the tawny sands and dark grey waters of Embleton Bay against that falcon's head of his.

The social attractions of the Northumbrian parish were singularly many. Creighton found himself in the centre of a bouquet of county families, not a few of which preserved in the present the fine traditions of a long hospitable past. The county called, of course, on the new vicar, and was not slow to discover that he was a man of power and charm. But there were two of the acquaintances so formed which ripened rapidly into friendships of great importance to the Oxford historian. Some five miles south of Embleton vicarage lay Howick, the home of that veteran Whig statesman, the third Earl Grey, who survived until long after Creighton left Northumberland, and who died, at the age of ninety-two, in 1894. Much nearer, and within his own parish, he had as neighbour Sir George Grey of Falloden, Lord John Russell's Home Secretary, and father of the present Sir Edward Grey; he died in 1882. With these two aged politicians, of high character and long experience, Creighton contrived to form relations which in the case of the Falloden family became positively intimate. The old Lord Grey, although he welcomed the vicar and delighted in his conversation, lived somewhat above the scope of practical mortal friendship; but his nephew, the present earl—then the hope of politicians, and known as Mr. Albert Grey—was one of the most frequent visitors at the vicarage.

At Oxford Creighton had found it impossible to devote himself to sustained literary work. The life of the tutor of a college is so incessantly disturbed, so minutely subdivided, that it is difficult indeed for him to produce the least example of a work of "long breath." In Northumberland it was not that time was unoccupied—wherever Creighton was, there occupation instantly abounded—but it was at least not frittered and crumbled away with hourly change of duty. Hence, directly we find him at Embleton his literary work begins; and it is during those nine Northumbrian years that he appeals to us pre-eminently as a man of letters. He began with several little books, of the kind then much advocated by the historians with whom he had thrown in his lot, such as Freeman and Green. It was, in fact, for a series edited by Green that Creighton wrote his earliest published work, a little History of Rome, in 1875. The next year saw the publication of no fewer than three of his productions, two at least of which, "The Age of Elizabeth" and "The Life of Simon de Montfort," remain highly characteristic specimens of his manner. Meanwhile he was writing anonymously, but largely, in various periodicals, such as the *Saturday Review* and the *Athenæum*, to the last of which he was for twelve years a steady contributor. In a variety of ways he was labouring to secure the recognition of the new science of history as he had accepted it from the hands of Stubbs and Freeman.

His own *magnum opus* was all the time making steady progress, and in 1882 were published the first two volumes of "The History of the Papacy during the Period of the Reformation." Of this book the fifth and last volume was sent from Peterborough in 1894. It is a massive monument of learning; it is the work by which Creighton, as a pure man of letters, will longest be remembered;

it is such a solid contribution to literature as few scholars are fortunate enough to find time and strength to make. The scope of the book was laid down by himself: it was "to bring together materials for a judgment of the change which came over Europe in the sixteenth century, to which the name of 'the Reformation' is loosely given." He passed, in his five volumes, from the great schism in the Papacy to the dissolution of the Council of Trent. It cannot be said that Creighton's "History of the Papacy" is a very amusing work. It was not intended to entertain. It seems to leave out, of set purpose, whatever would be interesting, and it tells at length whatever is dull. It was Creighton's theory, especially at this early period, that history should be crude and unadorned; not in any sense a product of literary art, but a sober presentation of the naked truth. Yet even the naked truth about what happened (let us say) under Pope John XXII. should, one would have supposed, have been amusing. But Creighton was determined not to stoop to the blandishments of anecdote or the siren lure of style.

Busy as he was with literature all through these years, he found, or made, at Embleton as much to do as would have satisfied most country parsons. The temporal wants of his parishioners immediately attracted his attention. Embleton has a fishing suburb on the sea, called Craster. This was a fever-ridden village, sunken in dirt and negligence. Creighton, disregarding the growls of the indignant and suspicious fishermen, took it vigorously in hand, drained it, cleaned it, held services there, founded—what had never been dreamed of—a village school. We used to tell him that Craster was his spoilt child. He seemed to hover about it, washing its unwilling face, and combing its wilful tangles. One watched him pounce down to see what Craster was doing, and sweep along the street of it like a winged person, ready to castigate or caress. It was in the school at Craster that an incident occurred which illustrates the difficulties of rural education. Creighton, who had been holding forth on the errors of ordinary teaching, took a London friend into the school at Craster to show how sensible and practical the mode was there. A mixed and straggling class came up, and the vicar asked the top pupil what is "the female of gander." One blank face was followed by another, until far down the class a dear little girl put forth a hand with "Please, sir, *gandress!*" Even Creighton, with all his humour, was not at first amused, but he consoled himself by thinking that it was "so like Craster."

But his duties and activities were not confined to the hamlets of his own large parish. He seemed at last to have the whole neighbourhood in his hands. He became the universal referee, the guide, philosopher, and friend of the whole of northern Northumberland. The county was in process of ecclesiastical reconstruction, and Creighton was made Rural Dean of Alnwick to help carry it out. It was presently formed into a diocese, carved out of the Palatine of Durham, and Creighton was the first Honorary Canon of the new Cathedral of Newcastle. These titles were straws that marked the current of his useful zeal. By and by the duke consulted him in everything; the bishop did not stir without him. It almost seemed as though his ambition would be satisfied with this sense of local beneficence. At the age of forty he was content to be simply the most indispensable man-of-all-work in a province of Northern England. But he was not born to live and die a useful rural dean.

At no time of his life were the mental and moral faculties of Creighton more wholesomely exercised than during the latter part of his residence in Embleton. In after years he pressed too much into his life: he was always "on the go" at Cambridge, always rushing about at Peterborough, while in London he simply lost control of the brake altogether and leaped headlong towards the inevitable smash. At Embleton, with his parish and his extra-parochial work, his private pupils and his books, his Oxford connection as public examiner and select preacher, and all the rest of his intense and concentrated activity, the machine, though already going at a perilous rate, had not begun to threaten to get beyond the power of the strong and spirited rider to stop at will. I was lucky enough, at this very moment of his career, to have an opportunity of studying closely the character and habits of my friend. In 1882 one of my children was ordered to a bracing climate, and Creighton suggested that nothing could possibly brace more tightly than the bright Northumbrian shore. He found us lodgings in the village of Embleton, and we sojourned at the door of his vicarage through the closing summer and the autumn of that year. Thus, without presenting the embarrassment of guests, who have to be "considered," we saw something of our fierce, rapid, alert, and affectionate vicar every day, and could study his character and mind at ease. We could share his rounds, romp with his children and our own, and engage at nights in the formidable discipline of whist.

Of all my memories of those days—bright, hard, hot autumn days, with Creighton in the centre of the visual foreground—the clearest are those which gather about tremendous walks. He was in his element when he could tear himself away from his complicated parochial duties, and start off, with his mile-devouring stride, full of high cheerfulness, and primed for endless discussion of religion and poetry and our friends. He was a really pitiless pedestrian, quite without mercy. I remember one breathless afternoon, after hours upon the march, throwing myself on the heather on the edge of Alnwick Moor, and gasping for a respite. Silhouetted high up against the sky, Creighton shouted: "Come on ! Come on !" And it was then that anguish wrung from me a gibe which was always thereafter a joke between us. "You ought to be a caryatid," I cried, "and support some public building! It's the only thing you're fit for!"

He was particularly fond of driving or taking the railway to a remote point, and sweeping a vast round on foot, preferably along some river bed. Thus have we ascended the Aln, and thus descended the more distant Blackadder in Berwickshire, and thus have we skirted the infinite serpentings of the Till from Chillingham to Fowberry Towers. But of all the wild and wine-coloured Northumbrian streams, it was the enchanting Coquet which Creighton loved the best. Mr. Hamo Thornycroft reminds me of an occasion when he was staying with me at Embleton, and Creighton took us for a long day's tramp up the Coquet to Brinkburn Priory. The river rolls and coils itself as it approaches the sea, and to shorten our course, the future bishop commanded us to take off our shoes and stockings, and ford the waters. There was a ridge of sharp stones from bank to bank, with depth of slightly flooded river on either side. He strode ahead like a St. Christopher, with strong legs naked from the knee, but he did not offer to take us on his back. On strained and wounded feet we arrived at last at the opposite shore, only to be peremptorily told that we need not trouble to put on our shoes and stockings, since we should have to ford the river again, after just a mile of stubble. Gentle reader, have you ever walked a mile barefoot in stubble? When we reached the foaming Coquet again, the ridged stones of the ford seemed paradise in comparison.

Truly the caryatid of Embleton was forged in iron.

III

The call to leave the moors and sandhills of Northumberland came abruptly and in an unexpected form. A remote benefactor of the University of Cambridge, and of Emmanuel College in particular, Sir Wolstan Dixie, of Christ's Hospital, had left a considerable sum of money, which it was now determined to use by founding a chair of ecclesiastical history. In 1884 this chair was finally established, and all that remained was to discover the best possible first professor. A board of electors, which contained Lightfoot, Seeley, S. R. Gardiner, and Mr. Bryce, very carefully considered the claims of all the pretendants, and at last determined to do an unusual thing, namely, to go outside the university itself, and elect the man who at that moment seemed to be, beyond question, the most eminent church historian in England. That this should be Creighton offers interesting evidence of the steady way in which his literary and scholastic gifts had been making themselves felt. He was not the Cambridge candidate, but Cambridge accepted him with a very good grace. Accordingly he returned to academic life, and at the same time enjoyed the advantage of becoming familiar with the routine of a university other than that in which he was brought up. But, while he was a professor at Cambridge for seven years, and was all that time entirely loyal to his surroundings, Creighton was too deeply impressed by an earlier stamp ever to be other than an Oxford man translated to the banks of the Cam.

At the very same time that Creighton became Dixie Professor, the present writer was elected to a post at Cambridge, and for five years we were colleagues in the university. Creighton's position included the advantages of a senior fellow at Emmanuel College, and he had rooms there, which, however, he very rarely occupied. He took a house for his family about a mile out of Cambridge, in the Trumpington direction, and he did his best, by multiplying occasions of walking out and in, to keep up his habits of exercise. But he certainly missed the great pedestrian activities of Embleton. His lectures were delivered in the hall of Emmanuel College, and I believe that they were fairly well attended, as lectures go at Cambridge, by young persons of both sexes who were struggling with those cruel monsters, the History Tripos and the Theology Tripos. But this formed, I must not say an unimportant, but I will say an inconspicuous part of Creighton's daily life, which in a few months became complicated with all sorts of duties. The year after he came to Cambridge he rose a step on the ladder of clerical promotion by receiving from the Queen a canonry at Worcester Cathedral. After this, like the villains in melodrama, he lived "a double life," half in Cambridge, half in Worcester.

The year 1886 was one of marked expansion in

the fame and force of Creighton. In the first place, Emmanuel College nominated him to represent her at the celebration of the two hundred and fiftieth anniversary of Harvard College, and on this occasion he paid his first visit to America. This was an event of prime importance to so shrewd and sympathetic an observer. I remember that he expressed but one disappointment, when he returned, namely, that he had not been able to go out West. He was charmed with the hospitality and the culture of the East, but, as an historian and a student of men, he wanted to see the bed-rock of the country. One rather superfine ornament of Massachusetts society lamented to him that he must find America "so crude." "My dear sir," said Creighton, in his uncompromising way, "not half so crude as I want to find it. We don't travel over the Atlantic for the mere fun of seeing a washed-out copy of Europe." I recollect observing with interest that what Creighton talked of, in connection with America, when he returned, were almost entirely social and industrial peculiarities, neither blaming nor approving, but noting them in his extremely penetrating way.

It was in 1886, too, that he began the work by which he became best known to the ordinary cultivated reader, namely, the foundation and editorship of the *English Historical Review*, which he carried on for five years with marked success. Perhaps no single book has done so much as this periodical did, in Creighton's capable hands, to familiarise the public with the principles of our newer school of scientific historians. At the same time he was writing incessantly in other quarters. To the Cambridge period belonged the third and fourth volumes of "The History of the Papacy" (1887), as well as the "Cardinal Wolsey" (1888), and several volumes of a more ephemeral character. Already, in the last preface to the "Papacy," there comes an ominous note: "The final revision of the sheets has been unfortunately hurried, owing to unexpected engagements." Of the rush of "unexpected engagements" his friends were now beginning to be rather seriously conscious. Whatever was to be done, as of old Creighton seemed to be man-of-all-work to do it. One finds among his letters of this period the constant cry of interruption. He has been on the point of finishing this or that piece of work, and it is not done. "I had a bad day again yesterday," he writes me from Worcester, "as I was chartered to lionise the British Association over the cathedral. Why do all 'associations' resolve themselves mainly into ugly women with spectacles?" I see that some of his friends think that the Cambridge-Worcester period was a restful one; I cannot say that this is how it struck me at the time.

It closed, at all events, in 1891. Magee, the famous Bishop of Peterborough, was made Archbishop of York in January, and about the same time Creighton received from the Queen a canonry at Windsor. He left Worcester in consequence, but he never resided at Windsor, since, before he could settle in there, he was called to fill the vacant see of Peterborough. Here, then, at last, he had started upon the episcopal career which was to carry his fame so far. He did not accept the great change in haste, although he must long have been prepared for it. We have been told, on hysterical authority, that Creighton spent a day "in great grief, trying hard to find reasons which would justify him in refusing Peterborough." This, of course, is sheer nonsense; this is the sort of conventional sentiment which was particularly loathsome to Creighton. There was no question of "grief" with him, no ultimate doubt that he must one day be a bishop; but there was cause for very careful consideration whether this was the particular time, and Peterborough the particular place, or not. As a matter of fact, the appointment rather awkwardly coincided with the earliest intimation he had had that his iron constitution was not absolutely impermeable to exhaustion and decay. It was in April 1891 that he was first known to declare that he was "rather feeble from overwork," and before he entered upon his new duties he spent some time of absolute rest and seclusion at Lower Grayswood, the Haslemere home of his lifelong friend, Mrs. Humphry Ward.

He entered upon his episcopal duties, in fact, in no very high spirits. He took a dark view of this, as he supposed, the turning-point in, or rather the sword-cut which should end, his literary career. The first time that I saw him after his settling in to his new work—it was in the dim, straggling garden of his palace, late one autumn afternoon—almost the first thing I said to him was, "And how about 'The History of the Papacy'?" "There's a volume nearly ready for press," he replied, "but how am I to finish it? Do you happen to know a respectable German drudge who would buy the lease of it for a trifle?" "But surely you will, you must bring this book of yours to a close, after so many years! Your holidays, your odds and ends of time——" "I have no odds and ends—I ought to be at this minute arranging something with somebody; and as to my holidays, I shall want every hour of them to do nothing at all in. Do you know," he said, gripping my arm, and glancing round with that glittering aquiline gleam of his, "do you know that it is very easy not to be a bishop, but that, if you are one, you can't be anything else? Sometimes I ask myself whether it would not have been wiser to stay where I was; but I think, on the whole, it was right to come here. One is swept on by one's fate, in a way; but one thing I do clearly see—that is an end of me as a human being. I have cut myself off. My friends must go on writing to me, but I shan't answer their letters. I shall get their books, but I shan't read 'em. I shall talk about writing books myself, but I shan't write 'em. It is my friends I miss; in future my whole life will be spent on railway platforms, and the only chance I shall have of talking to you will be between the arrival of a train and its departure."

These words proved to be only in part applicable to Peterborough. For the first year his time seemed to be indeed squandered in incessant journeyings through the three counties of his diocese. But after the summer of 1892 he became less migratory, and indeed for long periods stationary in his palace. He had resigned the editorship of the *English Historical Review* into the hands of Samuel Rawson Gardiner as soon as he was made bishop; and for some years it seemed as though all literary work had come to a stop. But by degrees he grew used to the routine of his episcopal duties, and his thoughts came back to printer's ink. The fifth volume of the "Papacy" got itself published without the help of any "German drudge"; in 1894 appeared the Hulsean lectures on Persecution and Toleration; and in 1896 he published the most popular and the most pleasingly written of all his books, his charming monograph on Queen Elizabeth. Then came London, and swallowed up the historian in the active, practical prelate.

So far as the general public is concerned, the celebrity of Creighton began with his translation to the see of London, on the promotion of Dr. Temple to the Primacy in January 1897. It was in the subsequent four years that he contrived to set the stamp of his personality on the greatest city of the world, and to impress a whole nation with his force of character. The obituary notices which filled every journal at the time of his death abounded in tributes to his ability as Bishop of

London, and in anecdotes of his conversation and his methods in that capacity. He arrived in his monstrous diocese at a time of disturbance and revolt; he followed a prelate who had not troubled himself much about ritual. Creighton set two aims before him, in attempting to regulate his tempestuous clergy: he wished to secure "a recognisable type of the Anglican services," and "a clear understanding about the limits of permissible variation." How he carried out these purposes, and how far he proceeded in the realisation of his very definite dreams, are matters which a thousand pens can speak of with more authority than mine.

But he attempted the physically impossible, and he flung his life away in a vain effort to be everywhere, to do everything, and to act for every one. No wonder that Lord Salisbury described Creighton as "the hardest-worked man in England." His energy knew no respite. There should have been some one sent to tell him, as the Bishop of Ostia told St. Francis of Assisi, that his duty to God was to show some compassion to his own body. An iron constitution is a dangerous gift, and the Bishop of London thought his could never fail him. But all through 1899, in his ceaseless public appearances, at services, meetings, dinners, installations, and the like, one noticed a more and more hungry look coming in the hollow cheeks and glowing eyes. In the summer of 1900 he collapsed, a complete wreck in health, and after a very painful illness he died on January 14, 1901. The sorrow with which the news of his decease was received was national, and the most illustrious of the thousands who sent messages of sympathy was Queen Victoria, who, only eight days later, was to follow the great bishop whose career she had watched with so deep an interest.

IV

The character and temperament of Dr. Creighton were remarkable in many respects, and were often the subject of discussion among those who knew him little or knew him ill. There is a danger that, in the magnificence of the closing scenes of his life, something of his real nature may be obscured; that he may be presented to us as such a model of sanctity and holy pomp as to lose the sympathy which human qualities provoke. There is another danger: that, in reaction against this conventionally clerical aspect, the real excellence of his heart may be done less than justice to. I would, therefore, so far as it lies in my power, draw the man as I saw him during a friendship of six-and-twenty years, without permitting myself to be dazzled or repelled by the dignity which the crosier confers. To do this, I must go back to the original *crux* in the career of Creighton—his taking of orders as a young man at Oxford.

To comprehend the position, one must first of all recollect how very "churchy" Oxford was between 1860 and 1870. At that time, it will be remembered, there was scarcely any scope for the energies of a resident don unless he was a clergyman. It must be admitted, I think, that Creighton's nature was not so "serious" at that time as it steadily became as years went on. I am prepared to believe that he took orders to a great extent for college reasons. He had an instinctive love of training and teaching, and these were things for which a priest had more scope than a layman at Oxford. There is no use in minimising the fact that his going into the Church caused the greatest surprise among his friends, nor in pretending that at that time he seemed to have any particular vocation for the holy life. He was just a liberal— one would have said almost anti-clerical—don, of the type which had developed at Oxford towards the close of the sixties as a protest against academic conservatism. I remember that Pater, discussing Creighton about 1875, said to me, "I still think, no doubt, that he would have made a better lawyer, or even soldier, than priest."

Those who judged him thus overlooked certain features in his character which, even at this early period, should have emphasised Creighton's calling for the sacerdotal life. His intense interest in mankind, his patient and scrupulous observation of others, not out of curiosity so much as out of a desire to understand their fate, and then to ameliorate it—this pointed him out as a doctor of souls. And his extreme unselfishness and affectionateness—no sketch of his character can be worth a rush which does not insist upon these. He was always hurrying to be kind to some one, combining the *bonitas* with *celeritas*. Love for others, and a lively, healthy, humorous interest in their affairs, were really, I should say, the mainspring of Creighton's actions. Voltaire somewhere exclaims, " Il faut aimer, c'est ce qui nous soutient, car sans aimer il est triste d'être homme"; and Creighton, who combined something of Voltaire with something of St. John the Evangelist, would have said the same. It was on the love of his fellow-men that he built up the unique fabric of his ecclesiastical life.

And this brings us to the everlasting question, which never failed on the lips of critics of Creighton—Was he, as they say, "a spiritually-minded man"? This, too, I think we may afford to face with courage. In the presence of his lambent wit, his keenness of repartee, a certain undeniable flightiness in his attitude to many subjects which are conventionally treated with solemnity, a general jauntiness and gusto in relation to mundane things, it must be conceded that the epithet which suited him was hardly this. He lacked unction; he was not in any sense a mystic; we cannot imagine him snatched up in an ecstasy of saintly vision. Creighton's feet were always planted firmly on the earth. But if I resign the epithet "spiritually-minded," it is only that I may insist upon saying that he was "spiritually-souled." He set conduct above doctrine: there is no doubt of that. The external parts of the religious life interested him very much. He had an inborn delicacy which made it painful to him to seem to check the individuality of others, and this often kept him from intruding his innermost convictions upon others. But no one can have known him well who did not perceive, underlying all his external qualities—his energy, his eagerness, his practical wisdom, his very "flippancy," if you will—a strenuous enthusiasm and purity of soul.

As a preacher Creighton improved after he became a bishop. In earlier days he had been dull and dry in the pulpit; of all exercises of his talent, I used to think preaching the one in which he shone the least. But he was an interesting lecturer, an uncertain although occasionally felicitous orator, and an unrivalled after-dinner speaker. To the end his talent in the last-mentioned capacity was advancing, and on the very latest occasion upon which he spoke in public—at the banquet given by the Lord Mayor on the occasion of the completion of the "Dictionary of National Biography"—although his face looked drawn and wasted, he was as fascinating as ever. His voice had a peculiar sharpness of tone, very agreeable to the ear, and remarkably useful in punctuating the speaker's wit. On all ceremonial and processional occasions Creighton rose to the event. He could so hold himself as to be the most dignified figure in England; and this was so generally recognised that when, in 1896, the archbishops had to select a representative of the English Church to attend the coronation of the Czar, their choice instantly fell upon the Bishop of Peterborough. Accordingly he proceeded, in great splendour, to Moscow, and he did honour to the Church of England by being a principal feature of the show. He was not merely one of the most learned as well as perhaps the most striking of the foreign bishops present, but he was unquestionably the most appreciative. He made great friends with the popes and prelates, and he was treated with exceptional favour. The actual chapel where the coronation took place was very exiguous, and the topmost potentates alone could find room in it. It was not characteristic of Creighton, however, to be left out of anything, and the other foreign representatives, to their expressed chagrin, saw the Bishop of Peterborough march into the holy of holies without them, between two of the officiating archimandrites.

To those who never saw Dr. Creighton some picture of his outward appearance may not be unwelcome. He was noticeably tall, lean, square-shouldered. All through his youth and early middle-age his frame was sinewy, like that of a man accustomed to athletic exercises, although he played no games. His head was held erect, the cold blue-grey eyes ever on the alert. His hair was red, and he wore a bushy beard, which was lately beginning to turn grizzled. The clearness of his pink complexion and the fineness and smoothness of his skin were noticeable quite late on in his life. The most remarkable feature of his face, without doubt, was his curious mouth, sensitive and mobile, yet constantly closing with a snap in the act of will. Nothing was more notable and pleasing than the way in which his severe, keen face, braced by the aquiline nose to a disciplinarian austerity, lightened up and softened with this incessantly recurrent smile. Such, in outward guise, was one of the strangest, and the most original, and the most poignantly regrettable men whom England possessed and lost in the last years of the nineteenth century.

1901.

ANDREW LANG
1844-1912

ANDREW LANG

INVITED to note down some of my recollections of Andrew Lang, I find myself suspended between the sudden blow of his death and the slow development of memory, now extending in unbroken friendship over thirty-five years. The magnitude and multitude of Lang's performances, public and private, during that considerable length of time almost paralyse expression; it is difficult to know where to begin or where to stop. Just as his written works are so extremely numerous as to make a pathway through them a formidable task in bibliography, no one book standing out predominant, so his character, intellectual and moral, was full of so many apparent inconsistencies, so many pitfalls for rash assertion, so many queer caprices of impulse, that in a whole volume of analysis, which would be tedious, one could scarcely do justice to them all. I will venture to put down, almost at haphazard, what I remember that seems to me to have been overlooked, or inexactly stated, by those who wrote, often very sympathetically, at the moment of his death, always premising that I speak rather of a Lang of from 1877 to 1890, when I saw him very frequently, than of a Lang whom younger people met chiefly in Scotland.

When he died, all the newspapers were loud in proclaiming his "versatility." But I am not sure that he was not the very opposite of versatile. I take "versatile" to mean changeable, fickle, constantly ready to alter direction with the weather-cock. The great instance of versatility in literature is Ruskin, who adopted diametrically different views of the same subject at different times of his life, and defended them with equal ardour. To be versatile seems to be unsteady, variable. But Lang was through his long career singularly unaltered; he never changed his point of view; what he liked and admired as a youth he liked and admired as an elderly man. It is true that his interests and knowledge were vividly drawn along a surprisingly large number of channels, but while there was abundance there does not seem to me to have been versatility. If a huge body of water boils up from a crater, it may pour down a dozen paths, but these will always be the same; unless there is an earthquake, new cascades will not form nor old rivulets run dry. In some authors earthquakes do take place—as in Tolstoy, for instance, and in S. T. Coleridge—but nothing of this kind was ever manifest in Lang, who was extraordinarily multiform, yet in his varieties strictly consistent from Oxford to the grave. As this is not generally perceived, I will take the liberty of expanding my view of his intellectual development.

To a superficial observer in late life the genius of Andrew Lang had the characteristics which we are in the habit of identifying with precocity. Yet he had not been, as a writer, precocious in his youth. One slender volume of verses represents all that he published in book-form before his thirty-fifth year. No doubt we shall learn in good time what he was doing before he flashed upon the world of journalism in all his panoply of graces, in 1876, at the close of his Merton fellowship. He was then, at all events, the finest finished product of his age, with the bright armour of Oxford burnished on his body to such a brilliance that humdrum eyes could hardly bear the radiance of it. Of the terms behind, of the fifteen years then dividing him from St. Andrews, we know as yet but little; they were years of insatiable acquirement, incessant reading, and talking, and observing —gay preparation for a life to be devoted, as no other life in our time has been, to the stimulation of other people's observation and talk and reading. There was no cloistered virtue about the bright and petulant Merton don. He was already flouting and jesting, laughing with Ariosto in the sunshine, performing with a snap of his fingers tasks which might break the back of a pedant, and concealing under an affectation of carelessness a literary ambition which knew no definite bounds.

In those days, and when he appeared for the first time in London, the poet was paramount in him. Jowett is said to have predicted that he would be greatly famous in this line, but I know not what evidence Jowett had before him. Unless I am much mistaken, it was not until Lang left Balliol that his peculiar bent became obvious. Up to that time he had been a promiscuous browser upon books, much occupied, moreover, in the struggle with ancient Greek, and immersed in Aristotle and Homer. But in the early days of his settlement at Merton he began to concentrate his powers, and I think there were certain influences which were instant and far-reaching. Among them one was pre-eminent. When Andrew Lang came up from St. Andrews he had found Matthew Arnold occupying the ancient chair of poetry at Oxford. He was a listener at some at least of the famous lectures which, in 1865, were collected as "Essays in Criticism"; while one of his latest experiences as a Balliol undergraduate was hearing Matthew Arnold lecture on the study of Celtic literature. His conscience was profoundly stirred by "Culture and Anarchy" (1869); his sense of prose-form largely determined by "Friendship's Garland" (1871). I have no hesitation in saying that the teaching and example of Matthew Arnold prevailed over all other Oxford influences upon the intellectual nature of Lang, while, although I think that his personal acquaintance with Arnold was very slight, yet in his social manner there was, in early days, not a little imitation of Arnold's aloofness and superfine delicacy of address. It was unconscious, of course, and nothing would have enraged Lang more than to have been accused of "imitating Uncle Matt."

The structure which his own individuality now began to build on the basis supplied by the learning of Oxford, and in particular by the study of the

Greeks, and "dressed" by courses of Matthew Arnold, was from the first eclectic. Lang eschewed as completely what was not sympathetic to him as he assimilated what was attractive to him. Those who speak of his "versatility" should recollect what large tracts of the literature of the world, and even of England, existed outside the dimmest apprehension of Andrew Lang. It is, however, more useful to consider what he did apprehend; and there were two English books, published in his Oxford days, which permanently impressed him: one of these was "The Earthly Paradise," the other D. G. Rossetti's "Poems." In after years he tried to divest himself of the traces of these volumes, but he had fed upon their honey-dew and it had permeated his veins.

Not less important an element in the garnishing of a mind already prepared for it by academic and æsthetic studies was the absorption of the romantic part of French literature. Andrew Lang in this, as in everything else, was selective. He dipped into the wonderful lucky-bag of France wherever he saw the glitter of romance. Hence his approach, in the early seventies, was threefold: towards the mediæval *lais* and *chansons*, towards the sixteenth-century Pléiade, and towards the school of which Victor Hugo was the leader in the nineteenth century. For a long time Ronsard was Lang's poet of intensest predilection; and I think that his definite ambition was to be the Ronsard of modern England, introducing a new poetical dexterity founded on a revival of pure humanism. He had in those days what he lost, or at least dispersed, in the weariness and growing melancholia of later years—a splendid belief in poetry as a part of the renown of England, as a heritage to be received in reverence from our fathers, and to be passed on, if possible, in a brighter flame. This honest and beautiful ambition to shine as one of the permanent benefactors to national verse, in the attitude so nobly sustained four hundred years ago by Du Bellay and Ronsard, was unquestionably felt by Andrew Lang through his bright intellectual April, and supported him from Oxford times until 1882, when he published "Helen of Troy." The cool reception of that epic by the principal judges of poetry caused him acute disappointment, and from that time forth he became less eager and less serious as a poet, more and more petulantly expending his wonderful technical gift on fugitive subjects. And here again, when one comes to think of it, the whole history repeated itself, since in "Helen of Troy" Lang simply suffered as Ronsard had done in the "Franciade." But the fact that 1882 was his year of crisis, and the tomb of his brightest ambition, must be recognised by every one who closely followed his fortunes at that time.

Lang's habit of picking out of literature and of life the plums of romance, and these alone, comes to be, to the dazzled observer of his extraordinarily vivid intellectual career, the principal guiding line. This determination to dwell, to the exclusion of all other sides of any question, on its romantic side is alone enough to rebut the charge of versatility. Lang was in a sense encyclopædic ; but the vast dictionary of his knowledge had blank pages, or pages pasted down, on which he would not, or could not, read what experience had printed. Absurd as it sounds, there was always something maidenly about his mind, and he glossed over ugly matters, sordid and dull conditions, so that they made no impression whatever upon him. He had a trick, which often exasperated his acquaintances, of declaring that he had " never heard " of things that everybody else was very well aware of. He had " never heard the name " of people he disliked, of books that he thought tiresome, of events that bored him ; but, more than this, he used the formula for things and persons whom he did not wish to discuss. I remember meeting in the street a famous professor, who advanced with uplifted hands, and greeted me with " What *do* you think Lang says now ? That he has never heard of Pascal ! " This merely signified that Lang, not interested (at all events for the moment) in Pascal nor in the professor, thus closed at once all possibility of discussion.

It must not be forgotten that we have lived to see him, always wonderful indeed, and always passionately devoted to perfection and purity, but worn, tired, harassed by the unceasing struggle, the lifelong slinging of sentences from that inexhaustible ink-pot. In one of the most perfect of his poems, " Natural Theology," Lang speaks of Cagn, the great hunter, who once was kind and good, but who was spoiled by fighting many things. Lang was never "spoiled," but he was injured; the surface of the radiant coin was rubbed by the vast and interminable handling of journalism. He was jaded by the toil of writing many things. Hence it is not possible but that those who knew him intimately in his later youth and early middle-age should prefer to look back at those years when he was the freshest, the most exhilarating figure in living literature, when a star seemed to dance upon the crest of his already silvering hair. Baudelaire exclaimed of Théophile Gautier: "Homme heureux! homme digne d'envie! il n'a jamais aimé que le Beau!" and of Andrew Lang in those brilliant days the same might have been said. As long as he had confidence in beauty he was safe and strong; and much that, with all affection and all respect, we must admit was rasping and disappointing in his attitude to literature in his later years, seems to have been due to a decreasing sense of confidence in the intellectual sources of beauty. It is dangerous, in the end it must be fatal, to sustain the entire structure of life and thought on the illusions of romance. But that was what Lang did—he built his house upon the rainbow.

The charm of Andrew Lang's person and company was founded upon a certain lightness, an essential gentleness and elegance which were relieved by a sharp touch; just as a very dainty fruit may be preserved from mawkishness by something delicately acid in the rind of it. His nature was slightly inhuman; it was unwise to count upon its sympathy beyond a point which was very easily reached in social intercourse. If any simple soul showed an inclination, in eighteenth-century phrase, to "repose on the bosom" of Lang, that support was immediately withdrawn, and the confiding one fell among thorns. Lang was like an Angora cat, whose gentleness and soft fur, and general aspect of pure amenity, invite to caresses, which are suddenly met by the outspread paw with claws awake. This uncertain and freakish humour was the embarrassment of his friends, who, however, were preserved from despair by the fact that no malice was meant, and that the weapons were instantly sheathed again in velvet. Only, the instinct to give a sudden slap, half in play, half in fretful caprice, was incorrigible. No one among Lang's intimate friends but had suffered from this feline impulse, which did not spare even the serenity of Robert Louis Stevenson. But, tiresome as it sometimes was, this irritable humour seldom cost Lang a friend who was worth preserving. Those who really knew him recognised that he was always shy and usually tired.

His own swift spirit never brooded upon an offence, and could not conceive that any one else should mind what he himself minded so little and forgot so soon. Impressions swept over him very rapidly, and injuries passed completely out of his memory. Indeed, all his emotions were too fleeting, and in this there was something fairy-like; quick and keen and blithe as he was, he did not seem altogether like an ordinary mortal, nor could the appeal to gross human experience be made to him with much chance of success. This, doubtless, is why almost all imaginative literature which is founded upon the darker parts of life, all squalid and painful tragedy, all stories that "don't end well," all religious experiences, all that is not superficial and romantic, was irksome to him. He tried sometimes to reconcile his mind to the consideration of real life ; he concentrated his matchless powers on it ; but he always disliked it. He could persuade himself to be partly just to Ibsen or Hardy or Dostoieffsky, but what he really enjoyed was Dumas *père*, because that fertile romance-writer rose serene above the phenomena of actual human experience. We have seen more of this type in English literature than the Continental nations have in theirs, but even we have seen no instance of its strength and weakness so eminent as Andrew Lang. He was the fairy in our midst, the wonder-working, incorporeal, and tricksy fay of letters, who paid for all his wonderful gifts and charms by being not quite a man of like passions with the rest of us. In some verses which he scribbled to R.L.S. and threw away, twenty years ago, he acknowledged this unearthly character, and, speaking of the depredations of his kin, he said :

> *Faith, they might steal me, wi' ma will,*
> *And, ken'd I ony Fairy hill,*
> *I'd lay me down there, snod and still,*
>   *Their land to win ;*
> *For, man, I've maistly had my fill*
>   *O' this world's din.*

His wit had something disconcerting in its impishness. Its rapidity and sparkle were dazzling, but it was not quite human ; that is to say, it conceded too little to the exigencies of flesh and blood. If we can conceive a seraph being funny, it would be in the manner of Andrew Lang. Moreover, his wit usually danced over the surface of things, and rarely penetrated them. In verbal parry, in ironic misunderstanding, in breathless agility of topsy-turvy movement, Lang was like one of Milton's " yellow-skirted fays," sporting with the helpless, moon-bewildered traveller. His wit often had a depressing, a humiliating effect, against which one's mind presently revolted. I recollect an instance which may be thought to be apposite : I was passing through a phase of enthusiasm for Emerson, whom Lang very characteristically detested, and I was so ill-advised as to show him the famous epigram called "Brahma." Lang read it with a snort of derision (it appeared to be new to him), and immediately he improvised this parody :

> *If the wild bowler thinks he bowls,*
>   *Or if the batsman thinks he's bowled,*
> *They know not, poor misguided souls,*
>   *They, too, shall perish unconsoled.*
> *I am the batsman and the bat,*
>   *I am the bowler and the ball,*
> *The umpire, the pavilion cat,*
>   *The roller, pitch, and stumps, and all.*

This would make a pavilion cat laugh, and I felt that Emerson was done for. But when Lang had left me, and I was once more master of my mind, I reflected that the parody was but a parody, wonderful for its neatness and quickness, and for its seizure of what was awkward in the roll of Emerson's diction, but essentially superficial. However, what would wit be if it were profound ? I must leave it there, feeling that I have not explained why Lang's extraordinary drollery in conversation so often left on the memory a certain sensation of distress.

But this was not the characteristic of his humour at its best, as it was displayed throughout the happiest period of his work. If, as seems possible, it is as an essayist that he will ultimately take his place in English literature, this element will continue to delight fresh generations of enchanted readers. I cannot imagine that the preface to his translation of "Theocritus," "Letters to Dead Authors," "In the Wrong Paradise," "Old Friends," and "Essays in Little" will ever lose their charm ; but future admirers will have to pick their way to them through a tangle of history and anthropology and mythology, where there may be left no perfume and no sweetness. I am impatient to see this vast mass of writing reduced to the limits of its author's delicate, true, but somewhat evasive and ephemeral genius. However, as far as the circumstances of his temperament permitted, Andrew Lang has left with us the memory of one of our most surprising contemporaries, a man of letters who laboured without cessation from boyhood to the grave, who pursued his ideal with indomitable activity and perseverance, and who was never betrayed except by the loftiness of his own endeavour. Lang's only misfortune was not to be completely in contact with life, and his work will survive exactly where he was most faithful to his innermost illusions.

1912.

WOLCOTT BALESTIER
1861-1891

WOLCOTT BALESTIER

It was early in 1889 that, on an evening which must always remain memorable to some of us, two or three English writers met, at the house of Mrs. Humphry Ward, a young American man of business who had just made her acquaintance. Among those who then saw Wolcott Balestier for the first time were Mr. Henry James (soon to become his closest and most valued friend in England) and the writer of these pages. As I look back upon that evening, and ask myself what it was in the eager face I watched across the table-cloth which could create so instant a thrill of attraction, so unresisted a prescience of an intimate friendship ready to invade me, I can hardly find an answer. The type was not of that warm and sympathetic class so familiar in our race; neither in colour, form, nor character was it English. In later moments one analysed that type—a mixture of the suave colonial French and the strained, nervous New England blood. But, at first sight, a newly presented acquaintance gained an impression of Wolcott Balestier as a carefully dressed young-old man or elderly youth, clean-shaven, with smooth dark hair, thin nose, large sensitive ears, and whimsically mobile mouth. The singular points in this general appearance, however, were given by the extreme pallor of the complexion and by the fire in the deeply-set dark blue eyes; for the rest, a spare and stooping figure, atonic, ungraceful, a general physique ill-matched with the vigour of will, the extreme rapidity of graceful mental motion, the protean variety and charm of intellectual vitality, that inhabited this frail bodily dwelling. To the very last, after seeing him almost daily for nearly three years, I never could entirely lose the sense of the capricious contrast between this wonderful intelligence and the unhelpful frame that did it so much wrong.

Charles Wolcott Balestier had just entered his twenty-eighth year when first I knew him. He was born at Rochester, New York, on December 13, 1861. His paternal great-grandfather had been a French planter in the island of Martinique; his maternal grandfather, whom he is said to have physically resembled, was a jurist who completed commercial negotiations between the United States and Japan. Of his early life I know but little. Wolcott Balestier was at school in his native city, and at college for a short time at Cornell University, but his education was, I suppose, mainly that of life itself. After his boyhood he spent a few years on the outskirts of literature. I learn from Mr. W. D. Howells that at the age of seventeen he began to send little tales and essays to the office of the *Atlantic Monthly*. He edited a newspaper, later on, in Rochester; he published in succession three short novels; and he was employed in the Astor Library in New York.

All these incidents, however, have little significance. But in the winter of 1882 he made an excursion to Leadville, which profoundly impressed his imagination. The Colorado air was more than his weak chest could endure, and he soon came back; but two years later he made a second trip to the West, in company with his elder sister, and this lasted for many months. He returned, at length, through Mexico and the Southern States. The glimpses that he gained in 1885 of the fantastic life of the West remained to the end of his career the most vivid and exciting which his memory retained. The desire to write earnestly seized him, and it was in Colorado that the first crude sketch of the book afterwards re-written as "Benefits Forgot" was composed. Soon after his return to New York he became known to and highly appreciated by men in business, and in the winter of 1888 he came over to England to represent a New York publisher and to open an office in London.

Of his three full years in the latter city I can speak with some authority, for I was in close relation with him during the greater part of that time. He arrived in England without possessing the acquaintance of a single Englishman, and he died leaving behind him a wider circle of literary friends than, probably, any other living American possessed. He had an ardent desire to form personal connections with those whose writings in any way interested him—to have his finger, as he used to say, on the pulse of literature—and the peculiarity of his position in London, as the representative of an American publishing-house, not merely facilitated the carrying out of this ambition, but turned that pleasure into a duty. He possessed a singularly winning mode of address with strangers whose attention he wished to gain. It might be described as combining the extreme of sympathetic resignation with the self-respect needful to make that resignation valuable. It was in the nature of the business in which Balestier was occupied during his stay in England that novels (prose fiction in all its forms) should take up most of his thoughts. I believe that there was not one English novelist, from George Meredith and Mr. Thomas Hardy down to the most obscure and "subterranean" writer of popular tales, with whom he did not come into relations of one sort or another, but sympathetic and courteous in every case. He was able to preserve in a very remarkable degree his fine native taste in literature, while conscientiously and eagerly "trading" for his friends in New York in literary goods which were not literature at all. This balance of his mind constantly amazed me. His lofty standard of literary merit was never lowered; it grew, if anything, more exacting; yet no touch of priggishness, of disdain, coloured his intercourse with those who produce what the public buys in defiance of taste, the honest purveyors of deciduous fiction.

Balestier's ambition on landing, an obscure youth, in an England which had never heard of him was no less than to conquer a place of influence in the centre of English literary society. Within three years he had positively succeeded in gaining such a position, and was daily strengthening it. There has been no such recent invasion of London; he was not merely, as we used to tell him, "one of our conquerors," but the most successful of them all.

What was so novel and so delightful in his relations with authors was the exquisite adroitness with which he made his approaches. He never lost a shy conquest through awkwardness or roughness. If an anthology of appreciations of Wolcott Balestier could be formed, it would show that to each literary man and woman whom he visited he displayed a tincture of his or her own native colour. Soon after his death I received a letter from the author of "John Inglesant," to whom in the winter of 1890 I had given Balestier a letter of introduction. "The impression he left upon me," says Mr. Shorthouse, "was so refined and delicate in its charm that I looked back to it all through that terrible winter with a bright recollection of what is to me the most delightful of experiences, a quiet dinner with a sympathetic and intelligent man."

Our notices of the dead tend to grow stereotyped and featureless. We attribute to them all the virtues, all the talents, but shrink from the task of discrimination. But the sketch which should dwell on

Wolcott Balestier mainly as on an amiable young novelist cut off in the flower of his literary youth would fail more notably than usual in giving an impression of the man. Of his literary work I shall presently speak: to praise it with exaggeration would, as I shall try to show, be unwise. But all men are not mere machines for writing books, and Balestier, pre-eminently, was not. The character was far more unique, more curious, than the mere talent for composition, and what the character was I must now try to describe. He had, in the first place, a business capacity which in its degree may not be very rare, if we regard the whole industrial field, but which as directed to the profession of publication was, I am not afraid to say, unique. He glanced over the field of the publishing-houses, and saw them all divided in interests, pulling various ways, impeding one another, sacrificing the author to their traditions and their lack of enterprise.

Balestier dreamed great dreams of consolidation, at which those who are incapable of the effort of dreaming may now smile, if they will. But no one who is acquainted with details to which I must not do more than allude here will deny that he possessed many of the characteristics needed to turn his dreams into facts. He held in his grasp the details of the trade, yet combined with them an astonishing power of generalisation. I have never known any one connected with the art or trade of literature who had anything like his power of marshalling before his memory, in due order, all the militant English writers of the moment, small as well as great. There they stood in seemly rows, the names that every Englishman honours and never buys, the names that every Englishman buys and never honours. Balestier knew them all, knew their current value, appraised them for future quotation, keeping his own critical judgment, all the while, unbent, but steadily suspended.

To reach this condition of experience time, of course, had been required, but really very little. Within twelve months he knew the English book-market as, probably, no Englishman knew it. Into this business of his he threw an indomitable will, infinite patience, a curious hunting or sporting zest, and what may be called the industrial imagination. His mind moved with extreme rapidity; he never seemed to require to be told a fact or given a hint twice. When you saw him a few days later the fact had gathered to itself a cluster of associate supports, the hint had already ripened to action. I may quote an instance which has a pathetic interest now. In the autumn of 1889, fresh from reading "Soldiers Three," I told him that he ought to keep his eye on a new Indian writer, Rudyard Kipling. " Rudyard Kipling ?" he answered impatiently; "is it a man or a woman ? What's its real name ?" A little nettled, I said, "You will find that you won't be allowed to go on asking questions like those. He is going to be one of the greatest writers of the day."

Pooh, pooh!" Balestier replied, "now you are

shouting!" And no further reference was made to the subject. But three days later I found a pile of the blue Indian pamphlets on his desk, and within a week he had added the future collaborator in "The Naulahka" to the troop of what he used to call his "personal conquests."

No striking qualities, as we know, are without their defects. The most trying peculiarity of Wolcott Balestier was the result of his rapidity in decisive manœuvring. He had cultivated such a perfect gift for being all things to all men, discretion and tact were so requisite in his calling, that he fell, and that increasingly, into the error of excessive reticence. This mysterious secrecy, which grew on him towards the last, his profound caution and subtlety, would doubtless have become modified; this feature of his character needed but to become a little exaggerated, and he would himself have perceived and corrected it. There was perhaps a little temptation to vanity in the case of a young man possessed of so many secrets, and convinced of his worth as a confidential adviser. He "had the unfortunate habit of staring very hard at his own actions, and when he found his relations to others refining themselves under a calcium light, he endeavoured to put up the screen." These words from a story of his own may be twisted into an application that he never intended. In the light of his absolute and unshaken discretion, of his ardent loyalty to his particular friends, of his zeal for the welfare of others, this little tortuous foible for mystery dwindles into something almost too small to be recorded.

For the ordinary relaxations of mankind, especially for the barbarous entertainments of us red-blooded islanders, he had an amused and tolerant disdain. He rode a little, but he had no care for any other sort of exercise. He played no games, he followed no species of sport. His whole soul burned in his enterprises, in his vast industrial dreams. If he tried golf, it was because he was fond of Mr. Norris; if he discussed agriculture and Wessex, it was because that was the way to the heart of Mr. Thomas Hardy. Nothing came amiss to him in conversation, and he was so apt a learner that he would talk charmingly of politics, of wine, of history, even of the fine arts. But only three things really occupied his mind—the picturesque procession of the democratic life of to-day, the features and fortunes of his friends, and those commercial adventures for the conduct of which he had so extraordinary a genius.

It is by design that I have not spoken hitherto of his own literary productions. It would be easier, I think, to exaggerate their positive value than to overrate the value of the man who wrote them. The three novels which he published in America ("A Patent Philtre," 1884; "A Fair Device," 1884; "A Victorious Defeat," 1886) were the outcome of an admiration for the later novels of Mr. W. D. Howells, but they had not the merit even of being good imitations. Balestier was conscious of their weakness, and he deliberately set himself to forget them. Meanwhile the large issues of life in the West and its social peculiarities fascinated him. The result of his study of the Leadville of 1885 will be found in a novel called "Benefits Forgot," which was finished in 1890, and published in 1892. During the last year of his life Wolcott Balestier took to composition again with much fervour and assiduity. There is no question that his intimate friendship with so eager and brilliant a writer of tales as Mr. Rudyard Kipling, who, as is known, became his brother-in-law, was of vast service to him. The short stories of his last year showed a remarkable advance. There remains the part of "The Naulahka" which he contributed, but on this it is impossible here to dwell. What he might have done, if he had lived ten years longer, none of us can conjecture.

The melancholy task remains to me of telling how so much of light and fire was extinguished. He habitually overworked himself to such a degree, the visible mental strain was so obvious, that his health had long given us the deepest anxiety. I, for one, for a year had almost ceased to hope that he could survive. Yet it now appears, both from the record of his family and from the opinion of the German doctors, that there was no organic mischief, and that he might, in spite of his weakness, have lived to old age. He was overworked, but he never worried; he was exhausted, but he did not experience the curse of sleeplessness. In

November, however, after some days of indisposition, looking all the while extremely ill, he left London for business reasons, and went to Berlin. We heard of him a few days later as laid up in Dresden. His mother and sisters immediately went to him from Paris. The disease proved to be typhoid fever in a most malignant form, and on the twenty-first day, Sunday, December 6, 1891, he died, having not quite completed his thirtieth year. He lies buried in the American cemetery at Dresden, and our anticipations lie with him :

> *For what was he ? Some novel power*
> *Sprang up for ever at a touch,*
> *And hope could never hope too much*
> *In watching him from hour to hour.*

1892.

CARL SNOILSKY
1841-1903

CARL SNOILSKY
AND SOME RECENT SWEDISH POETS

SWEDEN has followed the general tradition of the northern countries of Europe in the history of its poetry. Its earliest writers of the seventeenth century cultivated the didactic verse then generally prevalent, and were mainly occupied in redeeming the Swedish language from roughness and barbarism. Such poets as Stjernhjelm and Samuel Columbus, contemporaries of Dryden, Malherbe, and Logau, offered to their readers little lyrical faculty and less imaginative passion; they tended to the diffuse, the verbose, the rhetorical, but they polished and sharpened the instrument, they made the language of their country one peculiarly well prepared for the variety and harmony of the poetic art. Later poets looked to France for inspiration; there was a Ronsardist period and an Augustan period. Under Queen Ulrika Eleonora, Pope and Addison became the arbiters of poetic elegance. The close of the eighteenth century saw the arrival of Bellmann, the improvisatore of dithyrambs, a lyrical writer of the highest originality. Then, like her neighbours, Sweden experienced a change of heart; she passed through the throes of conviction of classic sin, and conversion to romantic righteousness. And all this time her language was becoming more mellifluous, more exquisitely balanced and burnished, more dangerously perfect in its technical softness and smoothness.

For fifty years of the early nineteenth century the Swedes distinguished themselves in several of the highest branches of poetical literature. But by 1850 Tegnér, Geijer, and Franzén were dead, and the lesser men around them were growing old. Poets continued to appear, but they made less and less impression. Between 1860 and 1870 the decadence of Swedish verse was conspicuous, and many observers believed that it was fatal. The language seemed to have worn itself out, and its facile sweetness to have become mawkish. Of the writers of that time, few are now read or much remembered. Their poetry was orthodox in style and tone, optimistic, commonplace. The best of it was remarkable for beauty of form, and certain pieces have been kept alive, and will probably always exist, by virtue of their delicate workmanship. But these young bards lacked enthusiasm and energy; their pathetic and graceful verses had no force; they cultivated, often in compositions of very trifling melody, what they called "idealism," a pretty wilful ignorance of all the facts of life.

A natural consequence was that the ordinary sensual man lost interest in verse, and a consciousness of a lack of hold upon the public increased the mediocrity of the poets. An extraordinary prudishness, tameness, and sentimentality spread over all departments of Swedish literature, and it seemed very likely, in 1870, that poetry might cease to be read and then to be written. Those pale and pure verses, without evidence of passion or experience, which alone were in fashion, were felt to be absurd. In the midst of this decadence, as though to arrest its ravages, and to make a bridge over from one vivid age to another, there made his appearance a lyrical poet of unquestionable force and fire. This was Count Carl Snoilsky, of whom it is hard to decide whether he was the last of an earlier age or the precursor of a coming generation. He was, at all events, genuinely inspired. Up to that time the best colour in Swedish poetry had been but chilly, an arrangement of the hues of the arctic aurora. But Snoilsky—the young Snoilsky—was intoxicated with life and joy, clad with the vine and stained with the grape, a figure like one of the followers of Bacchus, "crown'd with green leaves and faces all on flame," in Keats' glorious ode. This is how Snoilsky appeared, about 1870, to those who watched the signs of the times in Swedish poetry.

This remarkable man was a Swede of Slav extraction, whose ancestors, Znojilsek by name, had emigrated from Carinthia in the early part of the seventeenth century. The family was presently ennobled, and became distinguished in Swedish diplomacy. The father of the poet was one of the most conservative of the peers in King Oscar I.'s Upper House. It was in an atmosphere of Toryism, of aristocratic etiquette, that Carl Johan Gustaf Snoilsky was born, in the parish of Klara in Stockholm, on September 8, 1841.[1] We note him, in passing, to have been the immediate contemporary of Thomas Hardy and of Austin Dobson in England, of Sully Prudhomme and of Heredia in France. The early life of Count Snoilsky was not distinguished from those of most young noblemen of fortune who are destined from childhood for the service of the State. He began, however, quite soon to rhyme, and at the age of twenty produced a volume of "Short Poems," under the pseudonym which he long preserved, of Sven Tröst. This collection is sentimental and melancholy; we see in it the influence of current Swedish verse and some imitation of Heine.

When, however, Sven Tröst had recovered from the infantile malady of sentiment which the publication of his first volume brought to a crisis, he rapidly developed in an independent direction. The lyrical work of that period in Sweden was concentrated in a company of friends, lovers of romantic false names, who were known as the Signatures. Among them Sven Tröst had taken his place, and he continued to contribute to their annuals and anthologies, without

[1] Karl Warburg, perhaps the first of contemporary Swedish critics, has published an admirable biography, "Carl Snoilsky, hans lefnad och skaldskap." (Hugo Gebers Forlag, Stockholm.)

recognising how completely he was breaking away from them in spirit. In 1862 he seems to have perceived, by the light of nature, the insipidity and flatness of the "idealism" then prevalent in Swedish literature, and to have determined to practise, if he did not preach, what he called "a healthy artistic realism." His second book, "Orchids," was a collection of fifty poems instinct with sunlight and joy, flushed with the beauty of youthful exuberance. Denmark was at this time far more richly endowed with lyrical writers than Sweden, and it was Snoilsky's good fortune to come under the influence of those enchanting Danish song-writers of an earlier school, Christian Winther and Bödtcher. This little book showed great advance.

In 1864 Snoilsky went to Italy for a residence of many months, and so completed his poetical education. He enjoyed a delicate robustness of health, a conscious glow of youth, and he seems to have cultivated at this time, with remarkable success, the cordial epicureanism which so peculiarly suits the Swedish nation. It took in him that pleasing tone of seriousness, of tender sobriety, which robs the pursuit of pleasure of all its coarseness. At this, the moment of his highest emotional and imaginative development, we see Carl Snoilsky a sensitive creature of quite irresistible charm, aglow in Nero's Golden House at Rome, brooding in an elegant melancholy under the cypresses at Fiesole, leading the revels at Nemi with cups of Alban wine, or bewitching the rugged Ibsen in his little smoky *osteria* of the Via

Tritone. All this time Snoilsky was living and writing poems, such poems as had not been sung before, at least in recent times, under the pallid aurora of a Swedish sky. No translation can do justice to the qualities of the verse which Snoilsky composed during this ineffable pilgrimage of youth.

If there be a touch of weakness in the volume of "Poems," of 1869, by which Snoilsky first became widely revealed to the public, it consists in a perhaps too dainty or comely conception of art, an unwillingness, even while coming closely into touch with the reality of nature, to accept anything which is sordid or ugly. Throughout Europe in that generation the best of the poets were infatuated devotees of beauty, and they prepared the way for an inevitable reaction in favour of ugliness. But the note of joy, of physical ecstasy, in the dancing verse of Snoilsky was like witchcraft. It intoxicated his readers, accustomed to the staid melancholy and affected undertone of his fellow-singers. He stood out in the colourless current literature of his country like a piece of scarlet. The opening stanzas of the book of 1869 struck the note which never wavered:

"I bring grapes, I bring roses, I pour out beakers of my young wine. Up every pathway, at every cross-road, I smite my resonant tambourine.

"I do not weary you out of all your patience with insipid visions from the house of dreams. I sing exclusively of what I have seen and felt by the aid of my own five wholesome senses."

And all this in a metre that swings and dances,

with its ripple of rhymes, like a breeze in the top of a pine-tree.

Snoilsky returned to Sweden, to be sent away again as *chargé d'affaires* to Copenhagen, where he formed a close friendship with the first of recent critics, Georg Brandes. The present writer, who was in Denmark soon after this date, recalls how enthusiastically Brandes spoke of Snoilsky, and how ardent were his hopes for a complete rejuvenescence of the poetic literature of the North in the person of the brilliant young diplomat. However, a series of unlucky personal relationships seems about this time to have interfered with the free development of Snoilsky's genius. He had married in 1867, but not happily, and his family vexed him with a persistent complaint that he ought not to publish verses, as this was an act "unbecoming in a nobleman." Such a pretension can excite nothing but laughter, yet was an indication of the absolute absence of sympathy which gradually drained the happiness out of a life made for amenity and joy. His early career as a poet closed with a volume of "Sonnets" in 1871, after which it was understood that he consented to bow to the anti-poetical prejudices of his family. These sonnets are acknowledged to be the finest hitherto published in Swedish.

Snoilsky's withdrawal from the poetic art was, however, even now, rather relative than positive. He was engaged on a translation of the Shorter Poems of Goethe ; and original compositions of his own appeared, although rarely, and with manifest signs of a cessation of the old fire and enthusiasm. He was unhappy, dissatisfied, and life no longer offered him its grapes and its roses. In the spring of 1879 Sweden was thrilled by the news that Count Carl Snoilsky had left Stockholm, throwing up all his appointments and engagements, and that he was accompanied in his flight to Italy by one of the leaders of aristocratic Swedish society, the Countess Ebba Piper. For a long time they were lost to the circle of their friends "more than if they had been dead." But in 1880, the way having been made clear for them, the intrepid lovers were married at Marseilles, and the oppression of the last ten years seemed to be removed from the poet's inspiration. Snoilsky entered on his second poetic period. His wife and he went over to Africa, and spent many months in a slow pilgrimage through Algeria and Tunis, returning to Italy and ultimately settling in Florence. In 1881 his "New Poems" revealed to Swedish readers what may almost be called a new poet, no longer a fiery, spontaneous, and dionysiac improvisatore, perhaps, but a bard completely master of a grave, sonorous instrument. Snoilsky wrote in a private letter at this time: "The art of poetry has hitherto been a game to me. Now I am more and more penetrated by a sense of its deep seriousness and significance, and by a conviction that it is the real business of my life."

Engaged in literary work, Snoilsky remained abroad, chiefly in Dresden, until 1885, when, after a visit to Finland, he was persuaded to return for a few weeks' visit to Stockholm. The warmth of the reception which he received startled and touched him. The students arranged a festival in his honour; the King—Oscar II., himself a poet of renown—was graciousness incarnate. But Snoilsky could not be prevailed upon to stay; Dresden, he declared, had become his home. However, the fascination of the Fatherland became more and more overpowering, and few years now passed in the course of which the Snoilskys did not visit Sweden. In the autumn of 1890 his Byronic exile of nearly twelve years came formally to an end, when the poet accepted the post of Chief Librarian in the Royal Library of Stockholm. He wrote but little, and but little of that in verse, after his return to settle in his native land. The remainder of his life, spent in the serene and regular performance of his duties, and surrounded by the affection of his friends, was uneventful. His health gave way, and he was removed to a nursing home, where he died on May 19, 1903.

Although Snoilsky lived far into the revival of Swedish literature, it cannot be said that he showed much comprehension of its aims or sympathy with its movement. That, perhaps, was more than could be expected from a man of his character and antecedents. His own style had been definitely formed in the sixties, and there was much in the intellectual revolution of the eighties which could not but be distasteful to him. With all the beautiful qualities of his art, Snoilsky was deeply impregnated with the epicureanism which was typical of cultivated thought in Sweden during his youth, and he was not inclined to embrace the violent and sinister innovations of Strindberg and his followers. About 1880, outside his own practice, the vogue of verse in Sweden rapidly declined ; the darkest hour lasted from 1885 to 1890, when Swedish poetry was nearer total extinction than it had been for a couple of centuries. The new poetry, which came into being about the year 1891, was manifested, almost simultaneously, in the works of three very great lyrical artists, in whose hands Swedish verse once more rose to its proper eminence. These three poets were Fröding, Levertin, and Heidenstam. It is worthy of notice that the exhibition of this new energy in Swedish poetry was almost exactly coincident with the return of Snoilsky from exile to take up his official duties at Stockholm.

Few writers defy translation into a foreign language more completely than Gustaf Fröding who combines with a conscious study of the methods of the Northern folk-song a spontaneous lyrical elaboration of language and a buoyancy of metre which make his poems as difficult as they are fascinating. Fröding, who was born in 1860, died on February 8, 1911 ; for ten years he was in the retirement of a hospital at Upsala. His brilliant and meteoric career was practically confined within the brief years from 1890 to 1898. "Guitar and Harmonica," " Flashes and Patches," and equally eccentric titles to Fröding's successive volumes of verse, indicate the irregularity of his taste, in which something of Burns is combined with more than a touch of Baudelaire, and with a wildness, sometimes very ghastly and sinister, which is wholly his own. But he is perhaps the most interesting purely lyrical writer of modern Sweden.

In Oscar Levertin there was less phosphorescence and more witchery; he was not such an improvisatore as Fröding, but a finer craftsman. He was a Jew of Frisian extraction, born in Ostergötland in 1862. He had attained great eminence as a prose-writer, particularly in historical criticism, before his superb talent as a poet was revealed in 1891 by the publication of his "Legends and Songs." This volume, which he wrote at Davos while waiting for what he believed would be a hopeless struggle with consumption, produced a great sensation in Sweden. It has been said that the new epoch in Swedish poetry dates from the appearance of that volume. Levertin's use of language is magical, and his lyrics give a poignant expression to those feelings of frustrated passion and disillusioned longing which are so characteristic of the latest generation of Northerners. Levertin died in Stockholm in 1906.

Verner von Heidenstam, who was born in 1859, was the author of early poems of great beauty and originality, but he has now become principally known as a prose-writer whose monumental simplicity and classic beauty of style leave him without a rival among his contemporaries. Per Hallström, born in 1866, was one of those who were started on their poetical career by the revival of 1891; but he has written very little verse. He is known as a novelist of singularly penetrative fancy, and as a master of detail in observation. The production of poetry, as we understand it, is not very abundant in Sweden to-day. The word *diktare*, like *dichter* in German, does not mean *poet* in our English sense, a writer in verse, but an imaginative author generally. A novelist is call a *diktare*. But the Swedish language has a word, *skald*, which seems to answer precisely to the English word *poet*. It is needful to remember this in dealing with Swedish literature, or offence may be given by denying the title of poet to very distinguished masters of prose.

The new literature of Sweden is largely naturalistic, but in the new poetry of Sweden there is more than a trace of mysticism, which gives a strange perfume to the realism of such austere writers as Strindberg and Hallström, as well as to the more romantic idealism of Verner von Heidenstam and Selma Lagerlöf. But, whatever their individual tendencies, these new writers, whether in prose or verse, distinguish themselves by the vigour and the novelty which they have reintroduced into the somewhat exhausted literature of their country; and in this admirable labour it is manifest that Snoilsky was the direct pioneer of them all.

1911.

EUGÈNE MELCHIOR DE VOGÜÉ

1848-1910

EUGÈNE MELCHIOR DE VOGÜÉ

IN these days, when competent literary work is carried out punctually and monotonously by a large body of more or less professional writers, something more than the technical excellence of what is written is needed to arrest our attention to the man who writes. The author must offer some salient characteristic, some definite mental colour or spiritual form, if he is to be disengaged from the mob of gentlemen who sweep carefully and briskly over a wide variety of subjects. There must be a concinnity; the parts of a man's talent, character, history, idiosyncrasy must be so fitted together as to present a harmonious and definite effect. In such a concinnity the work and person of the late Vicomte de Vogüé do present themselves. On the crowded literary stage somebody always made an appearance when it was he who entered; a blank is manifest now that he so suddenly and untimely quits it for ever. In the few words that follow, written before the leaders of critical opinion in France have had time to sum up his qualities, an effort will be made to say how that dignified and austere figure struck an English contemporary.

There was little in the person of Melchior de Vogüé to attract the idle curiosity of the crowd, and in consequence he was never one of the notabilities of the boulevard. He was independent, austere, rather cold in manner, aloof from the crowd. He offered no affectation for the journalist, no eccentricity for the caricaturist. There was that in his outer presence which transmitted feeling with difficulty. Full of *bonté* as he was, he could not give an impression of *bonhomie*. He was timid, reserved, and conscious of his moral and intellectual superiority; the unreasoning quality in his fellow-men never ceased to distress and alarm him. He was the head of the younger branch of an ancient family, which had, in times past, scarcely distinguished itself by anything except its pride; "l'orgueil des Vogüé" had always been a proverb. In the eminent writer who has now left us the family characteristic took the form of a dignified withdrawal from controversy. He would not strive nor cry, but his tall, stiff figure, his careful dress, his limpid, penetrating eyes, his hard voice with the odd break in it, all combined to testify to the imperious, dictatorial, and self-concentrated nature which good breeding and good taste held in a perpetual outward control. He gave a sustained impression of suavity and serenity The ideal of Melchior de Vogüé was one of pure, unimpassioned intellectuality. His central ambition was to rule by sheer mental predominance. He was

Eugène Melchior de Vogüé

not indifferent to the passions of the hour, but he preferred not to be drawn into their vortex. He was not insensitive to the sorrows of the world, but he was thoroughly determined to stand outside all the coteries which battled about them in the public arena. He meant to help, but it must be by means of a long arm from outside.

This is the external view of the grave and punctilious aristocrat who occupied so large a place in the literary life of his time, and with whom, however, even in Paris, nobody was ever known to take a liberty. The internal view will, doubtless, be presently expressed by numerous and ardent friends. Vogüé was a stoic, but beneath his moral austerity there glowed a humanity none the less attractive because it was veiled by reserve. This cold, stiff man, who rarely smiled, who moved upon his appointed way as though his head were in the clouds, possessed an inward serenity which was founded, not on egotism, but on tenderness of aspiration. His peculiar earnestness and power were intensified by that content,

> *surpassing wealth,*
> *The sage in meditation found,*
> *And walked with inward glory crowned.*

The subject of his meditation was the redemption of the spirit of man. He found that spirit walking in a dry place, and he pondered long on a mode of leading it back into the oasis of dreams. He was faithful in hope; sad, but never discouraged; it seemed better to do nothing than to do what was hasty or commonplace. At length his patience left him. He found that the soul was being stifled in the French culture of his day, and he undertook its resuscitation. He tore away the cere-clothes of pseudo-scientific dogmatism, and he wrote (in his manifesto of 1885):

"A quoi bon vivre, si ce n'est pour s'instruire, c'est-à-dire pour modifier sans relâche sa pensée ? Notre âme est le lieu d'une perpétuelle métamorphose : c'est même la plus sûre garantie de son immortalité. Les deux idées ne sont jamais séparées dans les grands mythes où la sagesse humaine a résumé ses plus hautes intuitions."

This was strange language in the Paris of a quarter of a century ago, although it may seem natural enough to-day. If it is natural to-day it is largely because Melchior de Vogüé condemned the literary pharisaism which denied all modification and all intuition, and that jeered at the unseen and the unobserved. He is worthy of honour and attention because, in a dark hour, he stood out for loyalty, for religion, for hope and consolation. To him is due the reappearance of mystery and illusion in French imaginative literature. Weariness and emptiness had fallen upon the fields of literature, and it was Vogüé who called down once more upon them the dews of virtue and beauty. He has been called the Chateaubriand of the Third Republic, and the comparison is not without suggestiveness.

Marie Eugène Melchior de Vogüé was born at

Nice on February 24, 1848. Long afterwards, when he was admitted to the French Academy, it was whimsically remarked that, without close examination of the facts, no future historian would be able to decide whether he was born under a king or under a republic, in France or in Italy, a member of the nobility or a simple citizen. To these hesitations may be added another : whether his birthplace was really Nice by the accident of a visit, or the ancestral castle of Gourdan, where all his early life was to be passed. Gourdan, the home of the cadet branch of the Vogüé family, stands, deep in woods, near the summit of the Coiron, a chain of the Cevennes, in the wildest part of the wildest province of France, the Ardèche. Immediately around it the volcanic basalt takes shapes of grotesque and sinister violence, which filled the imagination of the child with wonder. From his mother, a very beautiful Englishwoman, who survived until 1910, Melchior obtained his earliest impressions of an exotic language and literature. He has described how, at a very tender age, he fell under the charm of the vast and deserted library at Gourdan, fitted out in the eighteenth century with everything proper for the boredom of a nobleman.

It was to another source, however, as he has told us in one of his rare moments of self-revelation, that he owed the bias of his life. He was taken, as a child, to see the curiosities of his own immediate neighbourhood, and these included, in that noble valley of the Rhone, the amphitheatres, aqueducts, triumphal arches, and ruined mausoleums of Roman Gaul. It was at Orange, or Nîmes, or Cavaillon that he felt "les premières secousses de l'âme," the earliest sensations of the majesty of the great dead past :

"Depuis lors" (he continues), "les hasards d'une existence errante ont fait relever les visions pareilles sous mes pas, au Colisée, à l'Acropole, dans les ruines d'Ephèse et de Baalbeck, sous les pylônes de Louqsor et sous les coupoles de Samarcande ; j'ai admiré partout, mais je n'ai retrouvé nulle part l'ivresse toute neuve, l'éblouissement laissé dans mes yeux par les reliques de Provence, par les blocs romains tremblants à midi dans la vapeur d'or, sur le pâle horizon d'oliviers d'où monte la plainte ardente des cigales."

Early he formed the design of becoming a traveller. It may strike us as strange that one who was to be the typically academic writer of his generation seems to have had no more regular education than could be given him, in a brief passage, by the Fathers of Notre Dame at Auteuil. At the age of twenty Melchior left "son château farouche" in the Ardèche and started wandering in Italy. There the war of 1870 found him. He rushed back to France and, in company with an elder brother, who was already commencing soldier at St. Cyr, volunteered for the front. He fought at Rethel, he was slightly wounded at Beaumont ; towards the close of the long and tragic day at Sedan his brother was shot dead at his side.

Melchior escaped, to be captured by the Prussians and imprisoned for six months at Magdeburg.

With his release his practical career began. His cousin, twenty years his senior, the Marquis de Vogüé —himself now a member of the French Academy— proceeded to Constantinople as Ambassador of the Republic, and Melchior, entering the diplomatic career, accompanied him as secretary. This was a period of awakening intellectual energy, the effects of which were manifest in all the young man's early writings, in the inevitable volume of poems, without which no prose-writer considers himself equipped (in Melchior de Vogüé's case never, I think, published), in his impressions of Syria, of Palestine, of Egypt, which were enclosed in his charming "Voyages au pays du passé" of 1876. It was at Constantinople that his soul was first roused to a clear perception of the eternal beauty of the past, and he spent, let us not say that he wasted, months and years listening to the waters of the Bosphorus as they broke in star-showers under the secular cypresses.

In the winter of 1872 he visited Ephesus, Rhodes, Byblos, Baalbeck, Jerusalem, everywhere intent upon following, as though it were a strain of fugitive music, the perpetual tradition of the past, everywhere seeking among the ruins of antiquity for the perennial melody of life. His earliest impressions are of a gravity which may almost make us smile, so little have they of the thoughtless buoyancy of youth. But the writer dreaded in himself as much as he detested in others the juvenile arrogance which breaks with bygone dignities. What he would have said to the Nathans and the Marinettis of to-day, the furious charlatans whose instinct before antique beauty is to shatter and defile, it is perhaps best that they should never know. The earliest essays of the Syria and Palestine series have the elegant *naïveté* of unconscious art. They would not have been written but for the accident that a friend, Henri de Pontmartin, who was prevented from accompanying Vogüé, begged for a detailed record, and, having received it, would give the author no peace until he had persuaded him to send his letters to the *Revue des Deux Mondes*. In the summer of 1875 Vogüé made a careful examination of Mount Athos, and the result of this was likewise welcomed by the *Revue*.

From Cairo Melchior de Vogüé was promoted to St. Petersburg in 1876. At the first shock the contrast between the South and the North seemed to be too severe, but he speedily regained his balance of spirit, and the problems of Russian history made a passionate appeal to his curiosity. He taught himself the Russian language, in which he presently became a proficient, and he threw himself with vehemence into the study of a people which was just beginning to attract warm sympathy in France, but of whose literature, customs, and traditions the French were still almost entirely ignorant. In Russia Vogüé found much ready help and many suggestions. He buried himself in the vast history of Soloviov, who was still alive, and, unless I am misinformed, he found occasion to attend the lectures of that eminent professor at Moscow. He followed with keen attention the archæographic and ethnographic discoveries of Kostmaroff, with whose enlightened and patriotic liberalism Vogüé was in full conformity. He was led on to study the Russian character as it is revealed by the great imaginative writers of the third quarter of last century, the giants who, at the time of his arrival in St. Petersburg, were, with the exception of Gogol, all still alive and at the height of their power.

It was part of the remarkable talent of Melchior de Vogüé that he was always ready to accept a new view of life. He was keen to appreciate all forms of vital beauty, however foreign they might be to the traditions in which he himself had hitherto been brought up. His spirit was from its birth a wanderer, but it traversed the waste places of the world without a trace of the brand of Cain upon its brow. On the contrary, the shadow of the pale leaf of the olive was always flickering against it. Vogüé, taking himself, as he did, infinitely *au sérieux*, very deeply interested in all the modifications of human life, already dreaming of how he might restore serenity and faith to the outworn intellectuality of France, was for a moment daunted by the strangeness of Russia, and then violently, and finally, fell in love with its indulgence and simplicity. In certain admirable recent studies[1] one of the best equipped of our younger critics has dwelt on the great difficulty presented by "the paradoxical thread which runs through the Russian character." Thirty-five years ago this element of paradox was unrecognised and undefined, even by the Russians themselves. It puzzled and baffled Vogüé, with his logical Latin instinct, his perfect reasonableness, his austere and authoritative temper of mind, but it rather fascinated than repelled him.

What we have to deal with here, however, is not the genius of Russia in itself, but the effect of that genius on the mind of a Frenchman destined, through his assimilation of certain elements in it, to exercise a great influence on his own people. Whether Vogüé really comprehended Russia or not is a question which I am not competent to answer, and it lies aside from the present discussion. What is interesting at this moment is the fact that a young French writer, resident in St. Petersburg between 1875 and 1882, carefully cultivating a rich, full style which he restrained within the limits of an almost classic purity, employed that style, with all its gravity of reflection and profusion of imagery, on the interpretation of an alien literature which was remarkable for the opposites of all these qualities, for turbulence, redundancy, stubbornness, exaggerated emotion, and sensuous extravagance of fancy. The strange material on which he worked

[1] "Landmarks in Russian Literature," by Maurice Baring. (Methuen & Co., 1910.)

not merely did not affect his method towards an imitation of itself, but the more intimately he studied it and extracted from it what was sympathetic to his temperament, the more were the eminently un-Russian qualities of Vogüé, his serried thought, the complication of his firm, ornate, rather old-fashioned style, his perfect probity and moderation of sentiment, emphasised in the careful progress of his writings.

It was in the presence of Russia that his own peculiar character became developed, one would affirm, in a peculiarly un-Russian direction. That he was absorbed, in these early diplomatic days, in the social forms and habits of his adopted country did not prevent him from remaining exquisitely and rigidly French. He traversed the vast empire from north to south; he followed the conquering army of General Annenkoff to Khiva and Samarkand; he even sealed his troth to Russia by marrying the general's sister, Anna Nicolaïevna, who, with their four sons, survives him to-day. In spite of all this, and in spite of the very strong infusion of Russian sentiment into his character and his strong streak of English blood, Melchior de Vogüé remained intensely French, and the principal result of his study of Russia was that his familiarity with the semi-Oriental order of ideas gave him a weapon to use in his approching fight in the West against the enemies of spiritual and religious beauty.

Vogüé's regular communication of Russian studies

to the *Revue des Deux Mondes,* with which he was identified until the end of his life, and from the office of which he may be said to have stepped into the French Academy, began in March 1879, upon the publication of his "De Byzance à Moscou." This rather abstrusely treated episode in Russian literature of the sixteenth century must have struck Buloz by its intrinsic merits, for it was given the first place in the review. It is noticeable that Vogüé, in describing the singular vision which appeared to the dying Czar Feodor in 1598, adopts the attitude towards the inexplicable, the mysterious, which he was about to make characteristic of all his writing. From this time forwards for more than thirty years we may trace in the pages of the *Revue des Deux Mondes,* in which most of his books originally made their appearance, the development of Melchior de Vogüé's critical powers, and their gradual progression, through archæology and history, to the analysis of pure literature and philosophical politics.

In 1882 he quitted the diplomatic career and returned to Paris, to devote himself without reserve to the practice of literature. On October 15 of the following year there appeared in the *Revue des Deux Mondes* the earliest of those studies of the Russian novel which, in their collected form, not only did more than anything else to make Melchior de Vogüé famous, but offered him an unanticipated opportunity for exercising a wide and salutary influence. It was about this time that he made the acquaintance of, or at least sealed his intimate friendship with, Taine, then at the zenith of his glory, and busily labouring at his colossal enterprise, the "Origines de la France contemporaine." It would not be exact to say that Vogüé became the disciple of Taine, for his own genius was by this time too mature for that, but the probity and profundity of the elder writer made a deep impression of encouragement on the mind of the younger. Vogüé was attracted to Taine by a considerable similarity in their temperaments; the younger man was by birthright what the elder had become under the stress of life, "majestueusement triste." They had a prodigious subject in common, the divagations of the human intelligence, its poverty and its weakness. Each had indulged, in the examination of life and history, an ardent curiosity; each had been easily persuaded of the preponderance of suffering and of the futility of contending with it otherwise than by a severe and patient stoicism.

Taine became to Vogüé a sort of living conscience. At the mere thought of any concession to the vulgarity of the crowd, the younger writer blushed beforehand at the silence of the elder. They exchanged impressions with regard to the foreign literatures which each of them loved more than did any other Frenchmen of their day; and Vogüé read the shorter tales of Tourgeniev aloud to Taine when the latter lay on his death-bed (March 1893). The account of Taine which Vogüé gives in his

"Devant le Siècle" has more human emotion in it than perhaps any other page of his work.

The native-born exile, returning to his fatherland, perceives alterations in thought and feeling more emphatically than those who have never stirred out of the environment of home. Melchior de Vogüé, coming back to Paris in 1882, was astonished to find the men of letters, his friends, comparatively oblivious of the strides which a positive utilitarianism had made during his absence. In the novel, in particular—that is to say, in the branch of literature which appeals most directly and most abundantly to the average emotional reader—the development of what was called "naturalism" had been extraordinary. Encouraged by the extreme favour with which the stories of the Goncourts and his own scientific and mechanical romances had been received by the public, Zola ventured on a policy of exclusion. He dared to close the doors of mercy on any novelist who presumed to admit into his work the least idealism, the least note of pity, the least concession to faith or conjecture. All must be founded on meticulous observation. The imaginative writer must be simply an "implacable investigator eager to take the human machine to pieces in order to see how its mechanism works." This scientific theory Zola expounded in three volumes of criticism, "Le Roman Expérimental" (1880), "Les Romanciers Naturalistes" (1881), and "Mes Haines" (1882). He bore down all opposition by his vehement sincerity, and he was much aided by the fact that for some years past all the cleverest young writers had been tending in the same direction, while the opposition of science to religion had been rapidly gaining ground in France. These were the years when the name of God was being erased from the school-books of Republican children, and when ardent provincial mayors were renaming Rue de Notre Dame de Bon-Secours, Rue de Paul Bert, or Passage de l'Adoration des Mages, Avenue de la Gare. These were the years when no valid resistance to the presumptuous and exclusive domination of logic seemed forthcoming in all the realms of French intelligence.

Vogüé, examining what had been published of late by the principal imaginative writers of France, protested that the soul had been forgotten. Zola was crying out, in his harsh and sincere voice, that the novelist must teach nothing but the bitter knowledge of life, the proud and unflinching lesson of reality. All pictures of society were to be painted without prejudice or sympathy, without comment, without effusion, in close agreement with what Edmond de Goncourt, in a famous phrase called " le document humain, pris sur le vrai, sur le vif, sur le saignant." There was a great deal to be said in favour of this cult of naturalism, which, reasonably followed, was doing wonders in clearing away the humbug, the dead flowers and last night's rouge, from an outworn romanticism. There could never be a return to the old romantic egoism, to a

series of pseudo-biographies of a generation of
Renés and Obermanns. The supreme value of
reality and the absolute necessity of observation
were admitted beyond all denial. But in the course
of his Russian studies Vogüé had discovered a school
of realists who were no less serious and thorough
than Zola, but who admitted far more spiritual
unction into their attitude to life. In Dostoieffsky
and Tolstoy he found great masters of fiction who
appreciated the value of scientific truth, but who
were not content to move a step in the pursuit of it
without being attended by pity and hope.

In 1883 Melchior de Vogüé began to print his
series of studies of the Russian novel in the
pages of the *Revue*. He treated Gogol, Tourgeniev,
Dostoieffsky, and Tolstoy; he traced the origins of
the tree of which they were the consummate
fruitage; he showed how Pushkin, an enchanting
poet, had made the ground ready for these giants in
prose. The subject was not absolutely new, of
course, to French readers; it had been treated
learnedly and amply by such excellent authorities as
Leroy-Beaulieu and Rambaud. Some of the novelists
themselves were already in the hands of Parisians,
Gogol and the now semi-Parisian Tourgeniev in
particular. But the two greatest of all were practically unknown, and it was while Vogüé's successive
monographs were appearing in the *Revue des Deux
Mondes* that Dostoieffsky and Tolstoy were for the
first time competently rendered in French, and in
this language circulated through the instructed

Eugène Melchior de Vogüé

world. All over France there was running at that time an increasingly sympathetic curiosity concerning Russian thought and Russian manners. The articles of Vogüé gratified this thirst for knowledge, but it was not until they were reprinted in a volume that their full significance was appreciated.

It was by "Le Roman Russe," which appeared in the summer of 1886, that Melchior de Vogüé first became widely known, and the "Avant-Propos" with which that volume was launched on the waters of controversy is of all his writings the one which has exercised the most lasting influence. This critical preface to a contribution to criticism has the extraordinary value of a manifesto, put forth with equal passion and adroitness at the precise moment when the reading world was ready to accept it. Every circumstance connected with its publication was happy. The articles on Russian literature, spread over three years, had greatly increased the prestige of the writer; their success had led to the introduction to French readers of the principal Russian works described; those works had been read, were now being more eagerly than ever read, still with some bewilderment at their strangeness; meanwhile the naturalistic theory of fiction, pushed to extremities by Zola and his disciples, had begun to pall upon their admirers. France was ready for a new voice, a fresh wind of the spirit; every one was prepared to welcome a man daring enough to proclaim that we had had enough of these dry bundles of observations, this mechanical pursuit of purposeless phenomena: "Our living and mysterious flower, the genius of France, cannot be plucked by botanists who merely catalogue dead species in their *hortus siccus.*"

The remarkable effect caused by the publication of "Le Roman Russe"—perhaps the most epoch-making single volume of criticism issued in France during our time—was due to the unusual literary conditions acted on by the daring and the sagacity of a wise and fearless writer. The Naturalists had pushed too far their formula that we can know nothing but what we can see, and that the inexplicable is the non-existent. From the dry positivism of this law there seemed to be no appeal until Vogüé, who had studied the Russians so closely, claimed to have learned from them, if he had learned nothing else, that there could be no more barren error than to limit our affirmations by our exact and measured experiences. He considered the theory of mankind as the Goncourts and Zola conceived it, and he was courageous enough to declare it hopelessly incomplete. Beyond it, stretching away in infinite chequer of radiance and shadow, he pointed to the domains of dreamland, untracked, unsuspected by the authors of "Chérie" and "La Terre."

The original object of Vogüé in writing his studies of the Russian novelists had been to draw the two countries closer together by the interpenetration of the things of the spirit. He had worked in certain definite zones of thought, whence he had chosen typical individuals; he practically confined himself to the four greatest masters of Russian fiction. He treated each of these in the best biographical temper, the man illustrating the work, and both seen in relation to society. In the course of this inquiry certain features of Russian imagination had strongly impressed themselves upon him. Mr. Maurice Baring has recently defined for us the elements of the realism of the Russians, "their closeness to nature, their gift of seeing things as they are, and of expressing those things in terms of the utmost simplicity." He proceeds to say that this is "the natural expression of the Russian temperament and the Russian character." This realism Vogüé compared with the formal and mechanical realism of the French Naturalists, and it opened his eyes to the fallacies of the latter. He saw that the aptitudes of Tolstoy and Dostoieffsky included a moral inspiration which alone could excuse the harshness of the realistic method.

It had become the principle of literature in Paris about 1885 to ignore the mystery which exists about us, to repudiate the tiny parcel of divinity which every human being contains. Vogüé's answer to Zola's challenge was that we must, indeed, affirm nothing dogmatically with regard to the unknown world, but that we should so far let ourselves go as to be for ever trembling on the brink of it. Realism, he pointed out, became odious at the moment when the development of its dogma insisted on the exclusion from its work of the element of charity. Literature, instead of acting as a stony-hearted contemplator of wretchedness, should make suffering supportable by an endless flow of pity. Vogüé spoke out, loud and bold, against the men of letters who denied that literature should, in any case, have a moral purpose, and who covered with scorn the novelist that endeavoured to console and fortify humanity. Which of you, he said in effect, will dare to contemn Dostoieffsky, under whose gigantic shadow you all shrink to a puny stature? When Edmond de Goncourt talked about the immutable laws of beauty which demanded the experimental treatment, Vogüé replied that the eminent connoisseur was confusing a material thing, the technical beauty of execution, with a divine and spiritual grace. The great word came out at last, and the critic burned his ships—"the religious sentiment is, after all, indispensable."

When this had been said, there could be no length of daring to which the critic would not be expected to attain. He ventured to speak with severity of the high priest of Naturalism, of the mighty Stendhal himself. He did not scruple to accuse "La Chartreuse de Parme" of abominable dryness, nor to stigmatise "Rouge et Noir" as disastrous and hateful. What he disliked in these illustrious romances, and in the less weighty examples of their posthumous children, was the coldness and emptiness of their attitude to life. On the other hand, in some English novelists, and in particular in George Eliot, he found exactly what he wanted—realism, but realism expanded by tenderness. Vogüé's tribute to "Adam Bede" is the most beautiful which George Eliot ever received: "Une larme tombe sur le livre; pourquoi je défie le plus subtil de dire; c'est que c'est beau comme si Dieu parlait, voilà tout."

Such is the temper of "Le Roman Russe." Melchior de Vogüé's attitude to religion in this manifesto, and throughout the remainder of his works, was somewhat difficult to define, since he never defined it himself. He said that life only begins where we cease to understand it, and he strongly reproved the positive arrogance which denies the existence of the unseen and the unconfirmed. He was stout in defence of the essential value of faith, and he objected to an excessive dependence on what is concrete and logical. Yet he never pushed his tenderness of soul to the point of mysticism.

The manifesto of 1886 had a remarkable effect. From all sides supporters came forward, souls who had wandered in darkness under the night of Naturalism. Vogüé found himself persecuted by would-be disciples, worried to lead down into the hurly-burly a self-styled body of "Neo-Christians." This was the absurd aspect of his influence; what alone he himself valued was the part he had been enabled to take in the revival of idealistic literature in France. He told his too ardent imitators, when they came to him for a creed: "You must choose your own mystery—the great thing is to have one." He probably hoped to see a definite reaction presently set in, not merely in literature, but in politics and manners, a return to classicism pure and simple, the undiluted *ancien régime;* but the democracy has grown too multiform and comprehensive for that.

During the quarter of a century which had succeeded his famous "Avant-Propos" the Vicomte de Vogüé lived a strenuous and uneventful life. In 1889 he was admitted into the French Academy; from 1893 to 1898 he sat in the Palais Bourbon as member for Annonay, the largest town, though not the capital, of his own department of the Ardèche. He travelled much; he made stately appearances in society; otherwise his whole career was concentrated in literature. He was a poor and proud aristocrat who made the writing of articles his profession. None of his books repeated the sensational success of "Le Roman Russe," but for all of them there was a loyal and respectful audience. In the midst of the frenzied *entente* of 1893 he published "Cœurs Russes," in which were the tales of Uncle Fédia, the colporteur, who gave his innocent life to save Akoulina; of Vassili Ivanovitch, the tyrant landlord who came to life again while the serfs were dancing round his death-bed; of Joseph Olénine and his magical robe of fur. He wrote novels, of which the best is "Jean d'Agrève," which has had passionate admirers, and which describes the life of a modern Tristram and Iseult in an elysian island somewhere off Hyères. This is marvellously written, but too lyrical to be quite successful as a novel; it is like what

"Epipsychidion" might have been if Shelley had written it in prose. One is surprised, on looking back, to see how many volumes the punctual and solid articles in the *Revue des Deux Mondes* contrived to fill as the years went uniformly by.

The Vicomte Melchior de Vogüé was a very brilliant writer, but he was even more remarkable as a man. He will be remembered because, when weariness had fallen upon the world of letters, he discovered an oasis with a magical fountain in it. He tasted very sparingly of that well of waters himself. He was austere, superficially dry, painfully haunted by the instability of things, chilled by the precarious and fragile tenor of all earthly hopes. But he was an idealist of the purest temper, and his loyalty, clairvoyance, and a certain majesty of mind were infinitely precious qualities in an age so chaotic as that in which we live.

1910.

ANDRÉ GIDE

ANDRÉ GIDE

INTERNATIONAL taste in literary matters is apt to be very capricious. France, well informed about Stevenson and Mr. Kipling, full of curiosity regarding Swinburne and Mr. Hardy, could not, to the day of his death, focus her vision upon the figure of George Meredith. These are classic names, but, among those who are still competitors for immortality, mere accident seems to rule their exotic reputation. The subject of the following reflections is an example of this caprice. He was born forty years ago ; his life has been, it appears, devoted to the art of writing, of which he has come to be looked upon in France as a master. In Germany, in Italy, he has a wide vogue, especially in the former. By a confined, but influential, circle of readers he is already looked upon as the most interesting man of letters under the age of fifty. But, so far as I have noticed, his name is almost unknown in England. This is the more extraordinary because, as I hope to suggest, his mind is more closely attuned to English ideas, or what once were English ideas, than that of any other living writer of France. He has reproved (in " Lettres à Angèle " and elsewhere) the "detestable infatuation" of those who hold that nothing speaks intelligibly to the French mind, nor can truly sound well in a French ear, except that which has a French origin. M. Gide has shown himself singularly attentive to those melodies of the spirit which have an English origin, but his own music seems as yet to have found no echo here.

Of the career of M. Gide little has been stated, since he is not one of those who talk freely about themselves in their books. But I take him to be a Southerner by extraction, born, or at least bred, in Normandy; an Albigense transplanted, with all his hereditary Protestantism, from Languedoc to the shores of the Channel. He says, somewhere, that the Oc and Oïl are equally familiar to his ear, and that he is not more devoted to the blossom of the apple than to that of the pomegranate. He has been, too, it is evident, a great wanderer over the face of Europe and Africa ("Amyntas"), and he affects, with an easy grace, some of the airs of the cosmopolitan. But in his heart I think that M. Gide is faithful to the Norman orchards. He is a product of Calvinism, and the extraordinary interest which the movements of his mind present is due to the concinnity they reveal in his moral basis. He offers himself to us, rather shyly, but very persistently, as a French Protestant who has grown up and out, oh! so far and so pathetically *out*, of the firm low root based upon the "Institution Chrétienne." As a rule, the products of French Protestantism have not much general value for an English reader.

Our race has gone so much further in that direction, and with so much more variety! The sacrifice of Calvinism to the national unity of the French has tended to dwarf the intellectual manifestations of the sect. But in the writings of M. Gide it is, I think, not too fantastic to discover what the importance of a Huguenot training can be in the development of a mind which has wholly delivered itself from the Huguenot bondage.

The progress of M. Gide has been slow. He attempted many things: sentimental autobiography, something after the fashion of Mr. A. C. Benson; poems in which he followed Laforgue and floated on the stream of symbolism; miscellaneous and extravagant tentatives, which were half prose, half poetry. Gradually he gained confidence. In 1899 his fantastic dream of a Prometheus in the Paris of our day was scornfully contested by the critics of the moment. In his curious dramas, "Saül" and "Le Roi Candaule," he felt his way towards a more and more personal mode of expression. He found it in his first serious novel, "L'Immoraliste," in his essays ("Feuilles de route," "Prétextes"), in his criticism. He has become what an early admirer prophesied that he would become, "a luminous Levite," one who with instant daily service tends the altar of intelligence and grace. He has gradually detached the singular originality of his temper from those accidents of style that enwrap, as silk enwraps a chrysalis, the formal parts of a new and ardent writer.

Among the early writings of M. André Gide, there is one which, to my mind, stands out prominent above the rest. It is as difficult to describe the element which makes "Paludes" (1895) one of the most exquisite of modern books as it would be to analyse the charm of "Tristram Shandy." People are fond of repeating that the French have no humour, but "Paludes" is humorous from end to end. It is not exactly a novel; it is rather a satire on the excess of introspection which leads clever young men to write novels when they have nothing of the least moment to communicate. It is the story of a person who had a false conception of life, who raised about him a whirlwind of painful agitation because he did not realise that but one thing is needful. The unnamed author searches for a subject, and hits heavily upon the notion of a Virgilian shepherd, a solitary Tityrus, who shall inhabit a tower in the midst of a marsh, a *palus*, and who shall cultivate his imagination there on the absence of every interest and object, in a vain search after originality. He starts upon his task, but the story—and no wonder—progresses at a snail's pace, interrupted by psychological digressions, checked by the depressing criticism of friends, and finally losing itself in a general vagueness and sterile melancholy. The solemn folly of the novelist is contrasted with the bustle, the insufficiency, the frivolity of the chattering companions who surround him, and there is not less satire of middle-class mental emptiness in these latter than of the pompous excess of intellectual pretension in the artist himself, tortured by his own self-consciousness. What makes "Paludes" extremely amusing to the consecutive student of M. Gide's work is that it marks a sort of crisis of good spirits, in which the youthful author turns suddenly upon himself with a burst of elfin laughter, and sweeps away the cobwebs of his own ingenuity. But the actual tissue of the book, with its swift alternations of beauty and fun, of malice and audacity, cannot be unravelled in a critical survey. "Paludes" lends itself, quite simply, to the pure enjoyment of the reader.

It is, however, in a novel of sober fullness and distinguished originality that M. Gide has now definitely risen above the level of what is merely ingenious, or fantastic, or suggestive. In "La Porte Etroite" (1910) he has written one of the most beautiful books which have been printed in Europe for a long time. It is, therefore, as the author of that noble story that I propose to dwell at some considerable length.

The scene of "La Porte Etroite" is laid in the neighbourhood of Havre, where there exists, and has always existed, a numerous Huguenot congregation. The hero of the story, who tells the tale, is the only child of an austere and melancholy, but passive widow; she and he share the company of a gentle English maiden lady, Miss Flora Ashburton, whose sunken fortunes have led her gratefully to accept this asylum. Between these pious gentlewomen Jérôme gradually develops from infancy to boyhood in a sheltered air. His only diversion is an occasional visit to his cousins, the Bucolins, who inhabit a large house, set in a great tumultuous garden, close by at Fougueusemare. The Bucolins are Protestants also, and worship at the Havre "temple," but their religion is not so sombre as that of Jérôme's household, and in their life there are exceptional circumstances. Uncle Bucolin is an active man, engaged in business, and Aunt Bucolin is more exceptional still, for she is a creole from Martinique, and she lies in bed half the day, and in a hammock the other half. The character of Aunt Bucolin has always been felt to be hostile to the heavenly calling, and as the years go by she becomes more reckless. The Bucolins have three children, the eldest of whom, Alissa, is two years older than Jérôme; Juliette and Robert are younger.

Jérôme cannot recollect a time when a kind of vague and seraphic attraction has not projected itself on his juvenile spirit from the presence and voice of his cousin, Alissa. She has developed, and is still developing, a delicate virginal beauty, of the Tuscan order. To the boy's innocent pedantry her pale oval face, and eyebrows tenderly arched, recall the vision of Beatrice. There is, however, no realisation of the nature of this feeling on his part until, one day, a singular set of circumstances combine to give it voice. In the unsuspecting absences of Uncle Bucolin on business, in the innocence of her two younger children, the creole aunt finds her opportunity to cultivate objectionable and dangerous acquaintances, and Jérôme is present at a "scene" when the lady from Martinique is guilty of an odious want of decorum. He flies to the room of his cousin, Alissa, who alone is conscious of the horror which surrounds them all, and who greets him, turning as she kneels in supplication at her toilet-table, with an agonised cry, "Oh, Jérôme, pourquoi reviens-tu?" He cannot understand, or but very vaguely divines, what is the cause of Alissa's beautiful anguish, but he feels the celestial purity of her sorrow; he interprets her cry as including him, adding his distress to the sum of humiliations; and this is the turning-point of his life. For the future the boy will exist for no other purpose than to fill the soul of Alissa with happiness and peace.

The terrible creole woman presently cuts the knot herself by disappearing with one of her lovers, and the Bucolin family never hear of her any more. Gradually they settle down again into their customary mode of life, their pious attendance on the means of grace, their cheerful relations with others, their mutual devotion. The sinful branch has been cut off; it has severed itself in a storm and been carried away in a night by the wind. At the chapel the incident is referred to, in the allusive manner customary among the devout, in the course of a powerful sermon on the text "Efforcez-vous d'entrer par la porte étroite!" The wide gate which leadeth to destruction is picturesquely described, and Aunt Bucolin, without actually being mentioned, is recalled to every mind as one of the noisiest of that over-dressed and loudly-laughing multitude which the preacher sees gaily descending to hell in the hideous exaggeration of sin. This remarkable discourse makes a profound impression upon Jérôme. He imagines himself, against his will, elbowed by the sin-stricken crowd, and stunned by the noise of its laughter. Each step he takes divides him further and further from the melancholy eyes of Alissa. Suddenly the preacher makes a new and a direct appeal: "Strive to enter in at the strait gate!" and dilates on the pure, the ineffable joy which streams from a life of self-abnegation, a life all devoted to sacrifice and holy sorrow. He compares this state of grace, this strenuous "walk with God," with an air played in a lovely garden on a violin, an ecstasy at once strident and tender. "Few there be," he exclaims, "who are chosen to pursue this life of sanctification." "I will be one of those few!" says Jérôme to himself. Looking across the pews of the chapel, he sees the pure countenance of Alissa all lighted up with the inward radiance, and he consciously unites, for the first time, the idea of her human love with that of the perfect love of Christ. He undergoes a double conversion; he gives his soul without reserve to God and to Alissa.

This conjunction of influences acts decisively on a spirit already prepared for it by the exercises of religion and by the puritan discipline of family life. As M. Gide very cleverly makes us feel, it is as natural for his hero to submit to moral restraints as it is for others to resist them. The instinctive habit of the circle in which Jérôme had been brought up was to seek for happiness where others seek for pleasure, and to find pleasure only in the Lord's service. But in spite of this condition of mind and heart, the world, with all its many-coloured show, is rapidly expanding before the lad, and he begins to comprehend, as many a pious youth has comprehended, that he cannot shelter his faith for ever behind the almost monastic hedges of private habit. In this crisis the love of Alissa seems to resemble the pearl of great price of which the Gospel speaks ; it is that for which Jérôme will cheerfully and even thankfully sell all that he has. It is with a hand of extraordinary firmness and delicacy that the author has drawn the years of adolescence, in which the nature of Jérôme widens and strengthens, without ever failing to keep the figure of Alissa before him like a star to guide him :

"Travail, efforts, actions pies, mystiquement j'offrais tout à Alissa, inventant un raffinement de vertu, à lui laisser souvent ignorer ce que je n'avais fait que pour elle. Je m'enivrais ainsi d'une sorte de modestie capiteuse et m'habituais, hélas ! consultant peu ma plaisance, à ne me satisfaire à rien qui ne m'eût coûté quelque effort."

But the interest of the story now centres in Alissa, of whom we ask, as Jérôme asks, what will be the development of her riper and perhaps intenser nature. Our first suspicion of a tragic destiny comes over us in the course of a scene, very lightly and even laughingly conducted, where Jérôme involuntarily overhears a conversation in the garden between his cousin and her father. Jérôme himself is the subject of their discussion, and his tendency to lean on the spiritual strength of others is animadverted upon. This leads to a talk between the cousins themselves, in which Alissa significantly asks him, "N'es-tu pas assez fort pour marcher seul ? C'est tout seul que chacun de nous doit gagner Dieu." She gently refuses to be his guide any longer: the soul can have no other guide but Christ. She winnows the vague grain of Jérôme's convictions, and his pious sentimentality is blown away in chaff by the steady breeze of Alissa's clearer theology. Still, he can but worship God in and through her. That, she replies, he must not do, for pure worship sees nothing between the worshipper and God Himself. This is the first little rift within the lute of their perfect unison of hearts, and it marks the difference upon which their happiness is to be ultimately shattered.

It would be to give a very false idea of this charming book to dwell to excess on the religious problem which it raises. The story is one of domestic provincial life in the north of France, among gentle and cultivated people, which is full of amusing studies of character, natural and entertaining incidents, and evidences of witty observation on the part of the author. But the real subject of the volume, the thread which runs through it and gives it intellectual adhesion, after all is precisely a searching analysis of the incompleteness and narrowness of the moral psychology of Protestantism. The author has seen how cruelly pietists suffer from excess of scruple, how disastrously they can be overwhelmed by the vain sentiment of sinfulness. He deals with a state of soul which is more comprehensible in English society than in French, and which has, perhaps, found no exponent before in the literature of France outside the ranks of those who have examined the results of a Jansenist training.

The family councils, while admitting that the ultimate marriage of Jérôme and Alissa is a matter of course, yet decide that a positive betrothal would be injudicious while Jérôme is so young. To this postponement the wishes of Alissa also tend, although the only scruple which she yet acknowledges is the result of her slightly greater age, and the tendency, which he continues to show, to lean unduly on her judgment. The reader is made to perceive that her character is much more fully developed, and set on a much firmer basis, than that of her cousin. Jérôme meanwhile proceeds into the world; he studies for a profession in Paris; he goes through his term of military service at Nancy; he engages in a long journey through Italy. All these events, by a natural process of experience, enlarge his intelligence, explain to him the meaning of life, modify his judgments on mankind. His pure and devoted passion for Alissa, nevertheless, is subject to no real diminution, although absence and physical change obscure and sometimes make difficult the expression of it. Moreover, it is now almost entirely restricted to correspondence.

While Jérôme sees the world, however, in all its variegated lights and colours, Alissa roams in the shadow of the garden at Fougueusemare. She is wholly occupied in being a mother to her old father and to his family, in attending to her charities, and in practising her religion. She grows neither sour nor bitter, but she becomes interpenetrated by the pangs of many exquisite scruples. The mother of Jérôme dies, and on her deathbed desires that she may see the hand of her son close in formal betrothal on the pale hand of Alissa; but the girl cannot persuade herself that she ought to bind her young cousin with any vow; she insists that they should wait until Jérôme is more sure of his own mind. "Comprends," she adds, "que je ne parle que pour toi-même, car pour moi je crois bien que je ne pourrai jamais cesser de t'aimer." At this moment, infinitely perplexing for the young lover, with his alternatives of docility and exasperation, the mind of Alissa is slowly proceeding in a direction still undetermined to her own consciousness.

From this point the relation between the lovers becomes more and more tragical. Various incidents, of a nature to enliven very agreeably and naturally the pages of M. Gide, interpose to prolong the inevitable delay, and to separate Jérôme still further from Alissa. These obstacles, however, seem to Jérôme to be exclusively of a material order; his fidelity to his purpose is unshaken, and he never ceases to regard his cousin as his guiding-star. Unfortunately, in the world of Paris and Italy, in the turmoil of literature and society, he finds the instinctive devoutness of his carefully guarded youth break down in an indifference which he deplores but scarcely tries to resist. Somewhere Renan makes a very acute remark when he says, in effect, "le plus grand nombre des hommes a besoin d'un culte à deux degrés." Jérôme, in the advancement of his years, rests more and more wholly upon Alissa for his religious preservation.

His cousin perceives this, and she retires from him. He must live for God by himself, or not at all, and in response to his passionate indignation, he receives a definite dismissal: " Adieu, mon ami. *Hic incipit amor Dei.* Ah! sauras-tu jamais combien je t'aime? Jusqu'à la fin je serai ton Alissa." The young lover, more ardent than ever, cannot but conceive that this is a trap laid for his too wary feet. In spite of prudence and duty, he will fly to protest to his cousin his entire, his unalterable ardour, and he will put an end to a false position, which scruples have made ridiculous, by insisting, at once, on a full and open ceremony of betrothal. He arrives, incontinently, at Fougueusemare, where the family receive him with enthusiasm, but only to find Alissa singularly changed. She avoids all private conversation with him, exhibits what in any one else would seem the evidences of coldness or disdain, and feigns—for it can but be feigning— to misunderstand every suggestion and every protest he makes. This mysterious situation culminates at length in another scene, at a subsequent and final visit to his uncle's house. Alissa now no longer shrinks from being alone with her cousin; she desires him to see her as she is. She presents herself to him very dowdily dressed, without any ornament; she takes him into her private room, whence all her pictures and her books have disappeared, "remplacés uniquement par d'insignifiants petits ouvrages de piété vulgaire pour lesquels j'espérais qu'elle n'avait que du mépris." He finds her altered in mind, in taste, in appearance; she has become wilfully colourless and dull; she has followed the cruel counsel of the theologian—*abêtissez-vous!* and to the protestations of Jérôme's anger and despair she replies with a gentle indifference. "'Laisse-moi vite,' dit-elle—et comme s'il ne s'était agi que d'un jeu : 'Nous reprendrons cette conversation plus tard.'"

The conversation is not resumed, and soon after this Alissa fades into a decline and dies. Her journals give evidence of a consuming passion for Jérôme, against which she has contended, vainly stoical, to the end. I do not know where to find elsewhere in recent fiction so pathetic a portrait of a saint as M. Gide gives us in Alissa Bucolin. She is like one of the religious women that the Sienese painters of the fifteenth century loved to represent, shadowless and pale, with the flame of sanctification already quivering on their foreheads; or like Santa Fina, as Ghirlandajo conceived her at San Gimignano, already lost to earth, "un fruit de souffrance" crushed into the cup of God's infinite mercy. But where the extreme skill of the author of "La Porte Etroite" is displayed is in the fact that while no element of Alissa's progress in holiness is caricatured or exaggerated, while every symptom of it is recorded with a perfect sympathy for herself and recognition of her aims, it is not with approval that M. Gide writes. We have not here a consecrated Huysmans vapouring about the ecstasies of St. Lydwine of Schiedam, but a man of modern training, clear-eyed and cool, who entirely appreciates the nature of the error he so closely describes, and regards it with deep disapprobation. The sacrifice which Alissa makes to scruple and to faith is a vain sacrifice, futile and wretched, a tribute to that religion "against nature, against happiness, against common-sense," which is the final outcome of Puritanism. But to all such arguments surely there is no better reply than the old, familiar one of William Johnson in " Mimnermus in Church " :

> *Forsooth the present we must give*
> *To that which cannot pass away;*
> *All beauteous things for which we live*
> *By laws of time and space decay.*
> *But oh, the very reason why*
> *I clasp them, is because they die!*

In 1911 M. André Gide presented to his readers a novel, "Isabelle," which is wholly unlike any of his previous books in character and form, yet which could only have been written by himself. This is a story of strange adventures, or rather the revelation of bygone adventures, in a decayed château of Normandy. Gérard Lacase, the supposed author of the tale, who is writing for his doctor's degree a thesis on the chronology of Bossuet's sermons, is informed that an old gentleman, member of the Académie des Inscriptions et Belles-Lettres, possesses—as people do in that wonderful France—a number of unpublished documents, and in particular a Bible covered with annotations by the very hand of Bossuet. Lacase obtains an introduction to this M. Floche, who lives in a country-house near Pont-l'Evêque, and in the middle of September he goes down, in response to an amiable invitation, to spend a few days at Quartfourche. His arrival is described in some of the most admirable pages that M. Gide has signed. Nothing happens as he expected that it would. The route is winding, interminable, aimless in the vague light of fading afternoon. The park, when the broken-down carriage, which has been sent to conduct the guest from the train, reaches it at last, is sombre, overgrown, and deserted. As Tennyson says:

> *He comes, scarce knowing what he seeks:*
> *He breaks the hedge: he enters there:*
> *The colour flies into his cheeks:*
> *He trusts to light on something fair.*

As a matter of fact, he lights on poverty, on eccentricity, on a baffling moral horror, the exposure of which, in a sense absolutely contrary to that which his young enthusiasm expected, gives the story its violent finale, its curiously disconcerting *dénouement*.

It would be manifestly unfair for me to spoil the legitimate surprise of the reader, which is led up to with an exquisite art. In fact, so far as the actual composition of "Isabelle" is considered, M. Gide has written nothing more instinct with his peculiar magic. Possibly, however, on laying it down, and on freeing himself from its immediate charm, the reader will be inclined to regard this novel as a step in the direction of M. Gide's enfranchisement from convention rather than as a work of positive perfection. It is an experiment in a mode hitherto unfamiliar to him. An effect more purely objective than had been produced in his earlier stories is here striven after. The subject being, as we say, objective, it is possibly a mistake to have told the narrative in the first person, since it involves an attitude in the narrator which is often not a little unbecoming. In order that the mystery should be unwoven, it is found needful that the young student of Bossuet should engage in a series of investigations which that meticulous prelate could not but have judged exceedingly indelicate. The young guest listens at key-holes, he spies out the movements of his hostesses, he opens and reads and acts upon a letter intended for no eyes so little as for his own. Probably, when M. Gide began his tale, he did not anticipate that it would be necessary to represent his young hero in the act of so many outrages upon good manners. He was intent on the psychology of his figures, upon the play of character under extravagantly unusual conditions. But this necessity, which involves the reader in some embarrassment, could have been avoided by a less personal method of delivery.

The cadences of M. Gide's prose are so delicious that I cannot resist the temptation to quote one more brief example chosen almost at random from his latest romance :

"Isabelle ! . . . et ce nom qui m'avait déplu tout d'abord, se revêtait à présent pour moi d'élégance, se pénétrait d'un charme clandestin . . . Isabelle de Saint Auréol ! Isabelle ! J'imaginais sa robe blanche fuir au détour de chaque allée ; à travers l'inconstant feuillage, chaque rayon rappelait son regard, son sourire mélancolique, et comme encore j'ignorais l'amour, je me figurais que j'aimais et, tout heureux d'être amoureux, m'écoutais avec complaisance. Que le parc était beau ! et qu'il s'apprêtait noblement à la mélancolie de cette saison déclinante. J'y respirais avec enivrement l'odeur des mousses et des feuilles pourrissantes. Les grands marroniers roux, à demi dépouillés déjà, ployaient leurs branches jusqu'à terre ; certains buissons pourprés rutilaient à travers l'averse ; l'herbe, auprès d'eux, prenait une verdeur aiguë ; il y avait quelques colchiques dans les pelouses du jardin ; un peu plus bas, dans le vallon, une prairie en était rose, que l'on apercevait de la carrière où, quand la pluie cessait, j'allais m'asseoir ; où, rêveuse,

Mademoiselle de Saint-Auréol s'était assise naguère, peut-être."

Among recent imaginative writers M. Gide is perhaps the most obstinately individualist. No subject interests him so deeply as the study of conscience, and in one of his early volumes I find this charming phrase, petulantly thrown forth to annoy the Philistines—"Chacun est plus précieux que tous." Nothing vexes M. Gide so much as the illogical limits which modern discipline lays down for the compression of the human will. He has written in "L'Immoraliste" what I admit is an extremely painful study of the irritation and misery caused by a too definite divergence from the comfortable type. He is impatient of the worry which is brought about by moral and religious abstractions, and this I take to be the central idea pervading some of his strictly symbolical work, such as the strange drama of "Le Roi Candaule" and the stranger extravaganza of "Philoctète." These are books which will never be popular, which are even provoking in their defiance of popularity, which, moreover, bear the stamp of the petulance of youth, but which will always attract the few by the remoteness of their vision and the purity of their style.

The strength of M. Gide's genius consists, I believe, in the delicate firmness of his touch as an analyst. He has no interest in groups or types; his eye is fixed on the *elected* spirit, on the ethical exception. One of his characters in "Le Prométhée Mal-Enchainé" exclaims, "Les personnalités, il n'y a que cela d'intéressant; et puis les relations entre personnalités!" We have here the strait gate through which the author takes all his imaginary figures, and if their conventionality has so flattened them out that they cannot pass the test, he flings them from him. It is a most encouraging matter to the admirers of M. Gide that his progress as an artist has been definite and steady. He has grown from year to year in his sense of harmony, in his sympathy with human existence. In his early books he gave a certain impression of hostility to ordinary life; his personal attitude was a little arrogant, tending a little to lawless eccentricity. The beautiful human pages of "La Porte Etroite" show how completely he has outgrown this wilful oddity of aim.

There is no other writer in Europe, at the present moment, whose development is watched with so eager an interest, by the most sensitive and intelligent judges, as is that of M. Gide. What will he do next; what will he grow into? Those are questions which every student of living literature must ask himself as he contemplates the author of "Prétextes" and of "Nouvelles Prétextes." He aims, we perceive, at giving a new direction to the art of the novelist, but who can feel sure that he has yet discovered the exact way in which this is to be done? Thus he is for ever experimenting; he is never satisfied, never content to be a *cliché* of himself. He seems to stand alone in the France of to-day, midway between the schools, now leaning a little to the revolutionary, now to the retrograde party. He is the opponent, I take it, of that rash and undisciplined improvisation which so dangerously fascinates so many young writers nowadays. On the other hand, he is not delivered up, bound hand and pen, to the old logical lucidity of classic France. There is something northern about his genius, which loves to cultivate tremulous caprices and the twilight hours, and dreads the excess of light that glares through the system of French intellectual discipline.

I have said that M. André Gide is more closely attuned in many respects to the English than to the French spirit. This is true, if we regard his attitude as a little belated. Since 1900 our native authors have adopted a vociferous tone, which is certainly not that of "La Porte Etroite." English literature has, in this twentieth century, set up a megaphone in the market-place, and the prize is for him (or her) who shouts the loudest. But when we say that M. Gide is in sympathy with English ideas, it is of a slightly earlier period that we are thinking. He is allied with such tender individualists of the close of the nineteenth century as Shorthouse and Pater. Those who delight in the contrast between types of character, exhibited with great dexterity by a most accomplished hand, will follow the literary career of M. André Gide with curiosity.

1909–12.

INDEX

INDEX

ACTON, Lord, 159
"Age, The," Bailey's, 88
"Age of Elizabeth," Creighton's, 177
"Angel World," Bailey's, 85
Arnold, Matthew, 155, 202, 203
Ashburnham, Lady Jane Henriette, 45
"Atalanta in Calydon," Swinburne's, 5-6

BAILEY, Philip James, 61-93. Parentage, 69; first edition of "Festus," 71; the "Festus" of 1901, 72; the lyrical element in "Festus," 73; the keynote of "Festus," 76; the narrative, 78; reviewers, 82; first admirers and advocates of "Festus," 84; "The Angel World," 85; "The Mystic," 87; "The Age," 88; style and influence, 85-93
"Balder," Dobell's, 91
Balestier, Wolcott, 215-225. Parentage, 216; early career, 216; life in London, 217-220; characteristics, 220-223
Baudelaire, Swinburne's review of, 5

"Bay of Seven Islands," Whittier's, 144
Bellmann, C. M., 229
"Benefits Forgot," Balestier's, 217, 224
Bigg, John Stanyan, 91
Benson, Mr. A. C., 217
"Blake, William," Swinburne's, 52
"Borough, The," Crabbe's, 146
"Bothwell," Swinburne's, 52
Brandes, Georg, 235
British Museum, 11, 130, 131
Browning, Elizabeth Barrett, 8, 42, 84, 112, 115
Browning, Robert, 54-55, 70, 130
Burton, Sir Richard, 32

"CARDINAL WOLSEY," Creighton's, 186
Carlisle, George, 8th Earl of, 6
Carlyle, Thomas, 65
Catullus, 37
Chambers, Robert, 89
"Chastelard," Swinburne's, 6
"Christian Year," Keble's, 156
Churchill, Randolph, Lord, 169, 170
Cladel, Léon, 56
"Cœurs Russes," Vogüé's, 264
Coleridge, S. T., 200
Columbus, Samuel, 229
Concord Riots, 141

"Cosmo de Medici," Horne's, 103
"Course of Time," Pollok's, 68
Crabbe, George, 145, 146
Creighton, Mandell, parentage, 166; at Oxford, 167, 177; characteristics, 167-169; at Embleton, 177, 182; at Cambridge, 183; in Peterborough, 186; in London, 189; at Moscow, 195; as a preacher, 194; person, 195; character and temperament, 191
Creighton, Mrs., 172
"Culture and Anarchy," Arnold's, 202

"Dead Love," Swinburne's, 5
de Vere, Aubrey, 61-63. Parentage, 119-210; characteristics, 121
de Vogüé, Eugène Melchior, 243-265. Person, 44-246; parentage, 246; early life, 247; travels, 248-250; talent, 251; Russian influence, 252-254; diplomatic career, 249-254; Taine, 255; in Paris, 256; studies of Russian novelists, 258-263; latest works, 264; "Revue des Deux Mondes," 254-265
Dickens, Charles, 47, 108-100
Dobson, Mr. Austin, 232
Dostoieffsky, 56
Dryden, 229
Dunton, Mr. Theodore Watts-, 53

"Earthly Paradise," Morris's, 203

Eleonora, Ulrika, Queen, 229
Eliot, George, 16, 263
Emerson, R. W., 140-141, 210
"English Historical Review," 185, 189
"Erechtheus," Swinburne's, 42
"Essays in Little," Lang's, 210

"Fair Device, A.," Balestier's, 223
"Fairy Tale, A," Bailey's, 88
"Faust," Goethe's, 72-74, 76
"Festus," Bailey's, 69-73
"Fifine at the Fair," Browning's, 54
"Flashes and Patches," Snoilsky's, 238
Franzén, F. M., 230
Freeman, Edward, 177
"Friendship's Garland," Arnold's, 202
Fröding, Gustaf, 238

Gainsborough, 152
Gardiner, S. R., 183
Gaskell, Mrs., 40
Gautier, Théophile, 35, 206
Geijer, E. G., 230
Gide, André, 269-289
Gifford, William, 145
Gladstone, W. E., 157, 159
Goethe, influence on Bailey, 74
Goncourt, Edmond de, 28
Gray, Thomas, 140
Green, John Richard, 177
Grey, George, Sir, 176
"Guitar and Harmonica," Snoilsky's, 238

Hallström, Per, 240
Hardy, Mr. Thomas, 218, 223, 269

Heidenstam, Verner af, 238
"Helen of Troy,' Lang's, 204
Hewlett, Mr. Maurice, 153
"History of the Papacy," Creighton's, 174, 176, 186, 188, 189
Holmes, O. W., 140, 141
Holy Grail," Tennyson's, 130
Horne "Orion," characteristics, 98-100; early adventures, 101; marriage, 108; in Australia, 109; his correspondence with Mrs. E. B. Browning, 100-115
Hugo, Victor, 31, 34, 40, 41, 203

IBSEN, 56
"Idylls of the King," Tennyson's, 129
"Immoraliste, l'," Gide's, 285
"In Memoriam," Tennyson's, 129
"Isabelle," Gide's, 282

JAMES, Mr. Henry, 215
"Jean d' Agrève," de Vogüé's, 264
"John Inglesant," Shorthouse's, 154-162
Jones, Sir Edward Burne-, 49
"Joseph and his Brethren," Wells's, 52
Jowett and Mazzini, 6

KEATS, John, 63, 101, 123, 231
Kipling, Rudyard, 221, 269

"LACON," Colton's, 64
Lagerlof, Selma, 240
Lamb, Charles, 53
Landor, W. S., 40, 44, 52, 53
Lang, Andrew, 199-211. Versatility, 200; individuality 202; eclecticism, 204; person, 206; wit, 209; temperament, 210
Leighton, F., 33
"Letters and Literary Remains," Shorthouse's, 151-152
"Letters to Dead Authors," Lang's, 210
"Lettres à Angèle," Gide's, 269
Levertin, Oscar, 238
"Life Drama, A.," Smith (Alex.), 91
"Little Schoolmaster Mark," Shorthouse's, 155
"Lucretius," Tennyson's, 129
Lytton, Sir E. Bulwer, 84

MACAULAY, Lord, 68
Malherbe, 229
"Manfred," Byron's, 72
Marston, P. B., 49
"Maud," Tennyson's, 129
Maupassant and Swinburne, 20-21, 27-31
Mazzini, 18
Meredith, George, 218
Milton, John, 209
Minto, William, 53
"Misérables, les," Hugo's, 40
Montgomery, James, 71
Morris, William, 42, 130, 155
Müller, Max, 172
"Mystic," Bailey's, 87

"NATURAL THEOLOGY," Lang's, 205
Newman, J. H., 122, 124-125
"New Poems," Snoilsky's, 236
"Night and the Soul," Bigg's, 91
"Night Thoughts," Young's, 81
North, Christopher, 124

"Old Friends," Lang's, 210
"Orchids," Snoilsky's, 233
"Orion," Horne's, 103–107
Oscar II., 237
O'Shaughnessy, Arthur, 49
Ossian, 63

"Papacy, History of," Creighton's, 174, 177, 186, 188, 189
"Paracelsus," Browning's, 69
Pascal, 205
"Patent Philtre," Balestier's, 223
Pater, Walter, 172, 288
"Philip van Artevelde," Taylor's, 66–69, 71
"Philoctète," Gide's, 286
Poe, Edgar Allan, 29
"Poems and Ballads," Swinburne's, 5–6, 36
Pope, Alexander, 229
Pope, John XXII., 178
"Porte Entroite," Gide's, 271–282
"Promethée Mal-Enchainé," Gide's, 286
"Prometheus," Horne's, 110
Purnell, Thomas, 53

"Queen-Mother," Swinburne's, 5

Ralston, W. R. S., 131, 133
Redesdale, Lord, 13
"Revue des Deux Mondes," 254, 258, 265
"Ring and the Book," Browning's, 54
"Roi Candaule," Gide's, 271
"Roman Russe, le," de Vogüé's, 263, 264
Romney, 152
Ronsard, 203–204

Rossetti, D. G., 39, 130, 155, 203
Ruskin, John, 153, 200

"Salathiel," Croly's, 68
Sartoris, Mrs., 33
Saturday Review, 177
"Saül," Gide's, 271
Seeley, Sir J. R., 183
Shakespeare, 41, 42
Shakespere Society, New, 54
Shelley, P. B., 24, 67, 82–83
Shorthouse, J. H., 151–162, 219, 288
"Short Poems," Snoilsky's, 232
"Simon de Montfort, Life of," Creighton's, 177
Smith, Henry, 172, 174
Snoilsky, Carl, 229–240. Parentage, 231; contemporaries, 232; early life, 232; in Italy, 233; in Sweden, 234; literary work, 236–239
"Songs Before Sunrise," Swinburne's, 6
"Songs in Time of Change," Swinburne's, 52
"Sonnets," Sir Aubrey de Vere's, 120
Southey, Robert, 65–67
Spasmodists, The, 91
Spectator, 5
Spedding, James, 132
Stevenson, R. L., 56, 207–208, 269
Stjernhjelm, 229
Swinburne, Adam de, Sir, 45
Swinburne, Admiral, 46–48
Swinburne, Algernon Charles, impression produced upon early admirers, 3; earliest works, 5–6; second period of public fame, 6; "The

Atalanta," "Chastelard," "Poems and Ballads," "Songs Before Sunrise," 6; physical conditions affecting genius, 8-15; unique appearance, 10; agility and brightness, 11; love of swimming, 12-13; characteristics, 14-15; Mazzini, 17-18; at Etretat, 19-28; with Maupassant, 20-32; at Vichy, 33; Victor Hugo, 34, 40-41; conversational powers, 36-39; study of Shakespeare, 41; the *Athenæum* and *Erechtheus*, 42; sentiment about literature, 43; intellectual temperament, 45; ancestry, 45; residence in London, 47; country home, 48; prodigious worker, 51; Browning, 54-55; Stevenson, 56; Ibsen and Dostoieffsky, 56; Zola, 56; Cladel, 56; revolt against the mid-Victorian Era, 57; praise of the sea, 175; Tennyson, 130
Swinburne, Miss Isabel, 14

TAYLOR, Sir Henry, 66
Tegnér, Esias, 230
Tennyson, Alfred, 84, 129-134
Thackeray, W. M., 84

Theocritus, 210
Thompson, George, 142
Thornycroft, Mr. Hamo, 132, 182
Tolstoy, 261
"Tom Jones," Fielding's, 154
Tourgeniev, 258
"Tracts for the Times," 65
Tröst, Sven, 232

VALLIN, Théodule, Capt., 23
Victorian Mid-Era, Swinburne's revolt against, 57
"Victorious Defeat," Balestier's, 223
Virgil, 119
"Voyages au Pays du passé," de Vogüé's, 249

WARD, Humphry, Mrs., 187, 215
Warburg, Karl, 232
Whistler, J. A. McNeill, 155
Whittier, J. G., 137-147. Person, 139; characteristics, 143; place as poet, 146
William IV., 64, 65
Winther, Christian, 233
Wise, Mr. Thomas J., 5
Wordsworth, W., 51, 65, 121-124, 157
"Wrong Paradise, In the," Lang's, 210

www.ingramcontent.com/pod-product-compliance
Lightning Source LLC
Chambersburg PA
CBHW020110010526
44115CB00008B/773